Investment and Reindustrialization in the Soviet Economy

Westview Replica Editions

The concept of Westview Replica Editions is a response to the continuing crisis in academic and informational publishing. Library budgets for books have been severely curtailed. Ever larger portions of general library budgets are being diverted from the purchase of books and used for data banks, computers, micromedia, and other methods of information retrieval. Interlibrary loan structures further reduce the edition sizes required to satisfy the needs of the scholarly community. Economic pressures on the university presses and the few private scholarly publishing companies have severely limited the capacity of the industry to properly serve the academic and research communities. As a result, many manuscripts dealing with important subjects, often representing the highest level of scholarship, are no longer economically viable publishing projects—or, if accepted for publication, are typically subject to lead times ranging from one to three years.

Westview Replica Editions are our practical solution to the problem. We accept a manuscript in camera-ready form, typed according to our specifications, and move it immediately into the production process. As always, the selection criteria include the importance of the subject, the work's contribution to scholarship, and its insight, originality of thought, and excellence of exposition. The responsibility for editing and proofreading lies with the author or sponsoring institution. We prepare chapter headings and display pages, file for copyright, and obtain Library of Congress Cataloging in Publication Data. A detailed manual contains simple instructions for preparing the final typescript, and our editorial staff is always available to answer questions.

The end result is a book printed on acid-free paper and bound in sturdy library-quality soft covers. We manufacture these books ourselves using equipment that does not require a lengthy make-ready process and that allows us to publish first editions of 300 to 600 copies and to reprint even smaller quantities as needed. Thus, we can produce Replica Editions quickly and can keep even very specialized books in print as long as there is a demand for them.

About the Book and Author

Investment and Reindustrialization in the Soviet Economy
Boris Z. Rumer

Investment activity in the Soviet Union is presently undergoing a decline hitherto unknown in the history of the nation: The growth of capital investment has stopped, while levels of production have fallen. One important factor in this phenomenon is the Soviet policy of reindustrialization—shifting new investments into the expansion and improvement of existing facilities—which severely limits capital available for new construction.

In this book, Dr. Rumer examines current Soviet investment policies and assesses their impact on economic development, especially in Siberia. Reindustrialization is intended to combine more rapid amortization for updating and retooling, growth in the volume of industrial output, and minimal capital investment. However, concludes Dr. Rumer, this investment pattern hinders the development of Siberia and thus reinforces the spatial polarization of fuel-energy and raw-material resources in the east of the country and the manufacturing industry in the west, with serious consequences for Soviet strategic/military vulnerability and for the Soviet economy.

Boris Rumer, previously head of the Department of Economics and Investment at the USSR Institute of Economics of the Construction Industry, is a research associate at the Russian Research Center, Harvard University.

To the memory of my father

Investment and Reindustrialization in the Soviet Economy

Boris Z. Rumer

Westview Press / Boulder and London

332.63
R865i

A Westview Replica Edition

All rights reserved. No part of this publication may be reproduced or transmitted in any form or by any means, electronic or mechanical, including photocopy, recording, or any information storage and retrieval system, without permission in writing from the publisher.

Copyright © 1984 by Westview Press, Inc.

Published in 1984 in the United States of America by
    Westview Press, Inc.
    5500 Central Avenue
    Boulder, Colorado 80301
    Frederick A. Praeger, Publisher

Library of Congress Cataloging in Publication Data
Rumer, Boris.
    Investment and reindustrialization in the Soviet economy.
    (A Westview replica edition)
    Includes bibliographical references.
    1. Capital investments—Soviet Union. 2. Soviet Union—Economic policy—1981– . 3. Capital investments—Siberia (R.S.F.S.R. and Kazakh S.S.R.). 4. Siberia (R.S.F.S.R. and Kazakh S.S.R.)—Industries. 5. Soviet Union—Industries. 6. Technological innovations—Soviet Union. I. Title.
HC340.C3R82   1984   332.63   84-7509
ISBN 0-86531-846-8

Printed and bound in the United States of America
10 9 8 7 6 5 4 3 2 1

And no one puts new wine into old wine-skins;
if he does, the new wine will burst the skins,
and it will be spilled, and the skins will be destroyed.

Luke V:36

CONTENTS

List of Tables	xi
Preface	xiii
Acknowledgments	xv

CHAPTER ONE: PATTERNS OF INVESTMENT ACTIVITY IN SOVIET INDUSTRY IN THE 1970s ... 1

Dynamics of Investment in the 1970s	1
Characteristics of the Investment Process	4
The Dynamics of the Capital Coefficient	6
Basic Factors Which Raise the Capital Coefficient	8
The Development of the Construction Sector of the Economy	10

CHAPTER TWO: RENOVATION VERSUS CONSTRUCTION: THE FOCUS OF INDUSTRIAL INVESTMENT POLICY   12

Priority Investment in the Renovation of Existing Enterprises	12
What Gosplan Means by "Reconstruction," and What Actually Happens	14
The Goals of Renovation and Their Realization	17
Maximum Investment in Equipment, Minimum Investment in Buildings and Structure	18
Why the Reconstruction of Old Buildings and the Construction of New Buildings Have Become So Widespread in the Course of Renovation	21
The Tempo and Qualitative Level of Equipment Renovation	25
Speeding Up Capital Turnover by Reducing the Amount of Time Needed for the Creation and Breaking in of Productive Capacities	33
Reasons for the Failure of the Reconstruction Policy	35
The Reduction in the Share of Net Investment and Some Theoretical Exercises on the Part of Soviet Economists	39

CHAPTER THREE: INVESTMENT PROBLEMS IN THE 1980s   47

The Main Features of the Investment Program for the First Half of the 1980s	47
Construction Challenges the Machine-Building Industry	52
Ameliorating Factors	53
Drawing Certain Analogies with the Past	55
Investments Must Climb for Industrial Output to Intensify	56
The Restructuring of Industrial Investments: The First and Foremost Condition for Industrial Growth	59

CHAPTER FOUR: THE EAST'S SHARE OF THE INVESTMENT
PIE AND THE ROLE OF SIBERIAN INDUSTRY. 65

 General Patterns of Change in the Spatial Structure of Capital
  Investment. 66
 The Fundamental Reasons for the Slow Investment Flow
  into the East. 74
 Underinvestment in Housing and Its Consequences. 79
 The Role of Siberia in Soviet Industry. 82
 Investment in Siberian Industry and Development of Oil and
  Gas Production. 85

CHAPTER FIVE: THE CONCEPT OF SIBERIAN INDUSTRIAL
DEVELOPMENT AND ITS IMPLEMENTATION. 89

 The Paradox of Electrical Energy. 91
 1. The Power Shortage in Siberia and Its Causes. 92
 2. The Kansk-Achinsk Node. 95
 The Paradox of the Machine-Building Industry. 101
 1. Trends in Siberian Machine-Building and Its Role in USSR
  Production. 101
 2. Lack of Correspondence of the Structure of Production to
  Requirements. 104
 3. Hypothesis on the Development of Siberian Machine-
  Building. 106
 4. Some Special Demands on Siberian Machine-Building Production. 110

CHAPTER SIX: PECULIARITIES OF CONSTRUCTION IN
SIBERIA. 114

 1. Underinvestment in Siberia's Construction Industry. 116
 2. The Absence of Construction Technology and Designs
  That Meet the Extreme Conditions of Construction
  on Northern Regions of Siberia. 117
 3. Retardation of Design and Industrial Construction Technology in the USSR. 120
 4. Impact of Obsolete Construction Technology on Siberia. . . 127
 5. Obsolete Forms of Organization of Construction. 131

General Observations. 134

CONCLUSION. 138

 Coda. 144

TABLES AND FIGURES

TABLES

1. The Relations of Increment in Output to Increment in Production Capacities. 34
2. Calculation of Actual Capital Expenditures on Replacement. 44
3. Extraction of Mineral Resources. 60
4. Comparative Economic Characteristics of the European and Asiatic Macrozones of the USSR. 66
5. Shifts in the Regional Distribution of Capital Investment as a Percentage of the USSR as a Whole. 68
6. Trends in Indicators Characterizing Spatial Shifts in Investment. .. 72
7. Shares of the European and Asiatic Parts in Industrial Output in the Late '70s. 73
8. Ratios of New Housing Construction to the Value of Fixed Capital Installed for the USSR and Major Zones. 80
9. Changes in Siberia's Share in the Economy of the USSR. 82
10. Growth of Gross Industrial Output in Siberia by Branch, 1961-75. 83
11. Planned and Actual Growth of Gross Industrial Output. 84
12. Growth of Fuel Production in Siberia. 87
13. Shares of Gas, Oil, and Coal in Siberian Fuel Production. 87
14. Siberia's Share in USSR Gross Output by Branch. 91
15. Siberia's Share in the Increments to Gross Output for the USSR by Branch. 91
16. Comparison of Growth Rates of Industrial and Machine-Building Output in the USSR and Siberia. 103
17. Basic Indicators for Machine-Building in the USSR and Siberia, 1961-75. 103
18. Branch Structure of Machine-Building in the USSR and West Siberia. 105
19. Distribution of Machine-Building in the European (Including the Urals) and Asiatic Part of the USSR. 110
20. Investment in the Construction Industry as a Share of Total Capital Investment. 116

FIGURE

1. Growth Trends in Soviet Capital Investment, 1965-80. 2

PREFACE

The Soviet Union, as well as the United States, is striving for reindustrialization, and its investment policy is subordinated to this goal.

For the USSR reindustrialization means a shift from the hypertrophied extracting and primary industries towards advanced industries. The more resources are diverted to production of raw and primary stage materials and fuels, the less can be allocated to production of new technology. This trend must be reversed if the Soviets are not to increase their dependency on the West for industrial innovation. But implementation of the reindustrialization takes place when investment activity is undergoing a period of decline unknown during the entire history of the USSR.

The investment mechanism is increasingly spinning its wheels. The growth of capital investment actually stopped, the volume of construction-installation work declined, the share of unfinished construction in capital investment attained a record level for the period since 1955, the growth of fixed capital stopped, and the amount of production capacity put into operation declined for most types of industrial production.

An even greater part of capital investment was channeled into replacement of machinery and equipment and the investment possibilities for expanding the scale of production and maintaining or increasing rates of economic growth declined correspondingly. Capital expenditures per unit increase in output continued to grow. All these phenomena are taking place simultaneously with a deteriorating demographic situation and a worsening of indicators characterizing the utilization of labor resources.

The key idea of reindustrialization under these conditions is the progressive shifting of investment flows into the development of existing production to the detriment of new construction. By this means it is proposed to combine more rapid amortization for updating and retooling industrial production facilities with growth in the volume of industrial output achieved through minimal capital investment.

The growing orientation of industrial capital investment toward the expansion and improvement of existing facilities hinders the solution of one of the most important tasks of the development of industry and the Soviet economy as a whole—the spatial deconcentration of industrial production and the creation of priority conditions for the industrial development of eastern regions of the country. Industrial enterprises in the western parts of the country, which produce 80 percent of industrial output, absorb more than 70 percent of industrial capital investment. With the increase in the share of reconstruction in capital investment, the investment quota of western regions also grows.

Such an investment policy increases the spatial polarization of the concentration of production of fuel-energy and raw material resources in the east and the production of manufacturing industry in the west, which has serious consequences for the economy of the USSR and increases its strategic-material vulnerability. Siberia, which is the center of economic development in the Asiatic part of the Soviet Union, is at the same time the focus of investment activity for the country as a whole. During the entire period of existence of the USSR, the Soviet leadership has always recognized the great significance of the intensive and comprehensive development of Siberia, both for the economy of the country and for military-strategic purposes. However, in practice the extent to which eastern and especially northeastern regions were provided with resources was always determined by some single narrow goal for which all else was sacrificed, putting the entire economic structure of a huge unsettled territory into the background. Stalin's proclaimed "law of planned proportional development of the economy," with respect to Siberia, can rightly be called the "law of disproportional and unplanned development of the economy." And in the Brezhnev period also, Siberia developed as a narrowly oriented part of the national economic system. Its development was like a swollen cheek.

Within this boundless topic, I will focus attention on the nerve centers of the contemporary industrial development of a huge region whose economic growth will determine to a decisive extent the rhythm and dynamics of the entire Soviet economy in the foreseeable future. Thus, the present work does not pretend in any way to an exhaustive treatment of investment problems or the problems of economic development in the eastern regions of the USSR, focusing instead on the key issues: power shortage, slow development of machine-building, and construction industry.

This monograph is based on data drawn from official Soviet statistical sources and articles and monographs published in the USSR. I evaluate the reliability of this sort of information completely realistically. However, in spite of all its shortcomings, in my opinion it reflects the basic trends, reveals structural changes and explains the essence of the phenomenon examined.

Boris Z. Rumer

ACKNOWLEDGMENTS

The research on which this book is based was carried out at the Russian Research Center of Harvard University. The warm and intellectually invigorating atmosphere of the Center, and the sympathetic attitude of its Director, Adam B. Ulam, and its Administrative Assistant, Mary Towle, greatly aided me in my work.

I was fortunate enough to have received two grants from the National Council for Soviet and East European Research. Without the Council's support, this work would not have been possible.

My special thanks go to Professors Abram Bergson, Evsey Domar, Vladimir Treml, and to Mr. Vladimir Toumanoff, for their help and encouragement.

I am also indebted to my colleagues at the Russian Research Center, Professors Joseph Berliner, Helen Boss, Gregory Freeze, Marshall Goldman, Loren Graham, Norman Naimark, Aleksandr Nekrich, David Powell, Herbert Sawyer, Barney Schwalberg, Stephen Sternheimer for their unstinting help.

I am beholden to Drs. I. Birman, J. Gillula and A. Tret'yakova for their valuable remarks.

Some sections of this text were previously published in a slightly different form in: *Soviet Studies, Problems of Communism, Berichte des Budesinstituts für ostwissenschaftliche und internationale Studien,* and *Harvard Business Review.* I would like to thank the editors of these journals for their permission to reprint this material.

Boris Z. Rumer

CHAPTER ONE

PATTERNS OF INVESTMENT ACTIVITY IN SOVIET INDUSTRY IN THE 1970s

> Strategically, from the point of view of solving fundamental problems, the reserves of operating plants are almost exhausted .... Under such conditions, there occurred an absolute reduction in the real dimensions of industrial capital investments between the ninth and tenth five-year plans.
>
> Prof. Konstantin Val'tukh,
> Siberian Branch, USSR Academy of Science

DYNAMICS OF INVESTMENT IN THE 1970s

The development of the Soviet economy since the second half of the 1970s differed qualitatively from earlier periods in that there was an absolute decline in the increments to capital and labor resources.

By the late 1970s, the pulse rate of Soviet economic investment had become so weak and irregular that it appeared scarcely capable of sustaining the steady flow of investment funds necessary for a healthy economy. The dynamics of national economic investment and volume of construction for the whole of Brezhnev's tenure are characterized in Figure 1.

The slump in investment activity which occurred in the late 1970s is entirely without precedent for a peacetime Soviet economy. This reduction of actual investment capabilities has resulted in an unprecedented curtailment of the introduction of productive capacities in all spheres of the economy. In the period 1976-80, only sixteen of the 54 kinds of new capacities recorded annually in published Soviet sources showed an increase over the period 1971-75, while 38 suffered a reduction. There were major reductions in such important and scarce products as rolled ferrous metals (40%), steel pipes (21%), turbines (46%), machine tools (200%), automobiles (almost 400%), cement (almost 300%), chemical fibers (35%), and footwear (more than 300%). The number of new capacities was significantly reduced in the production of

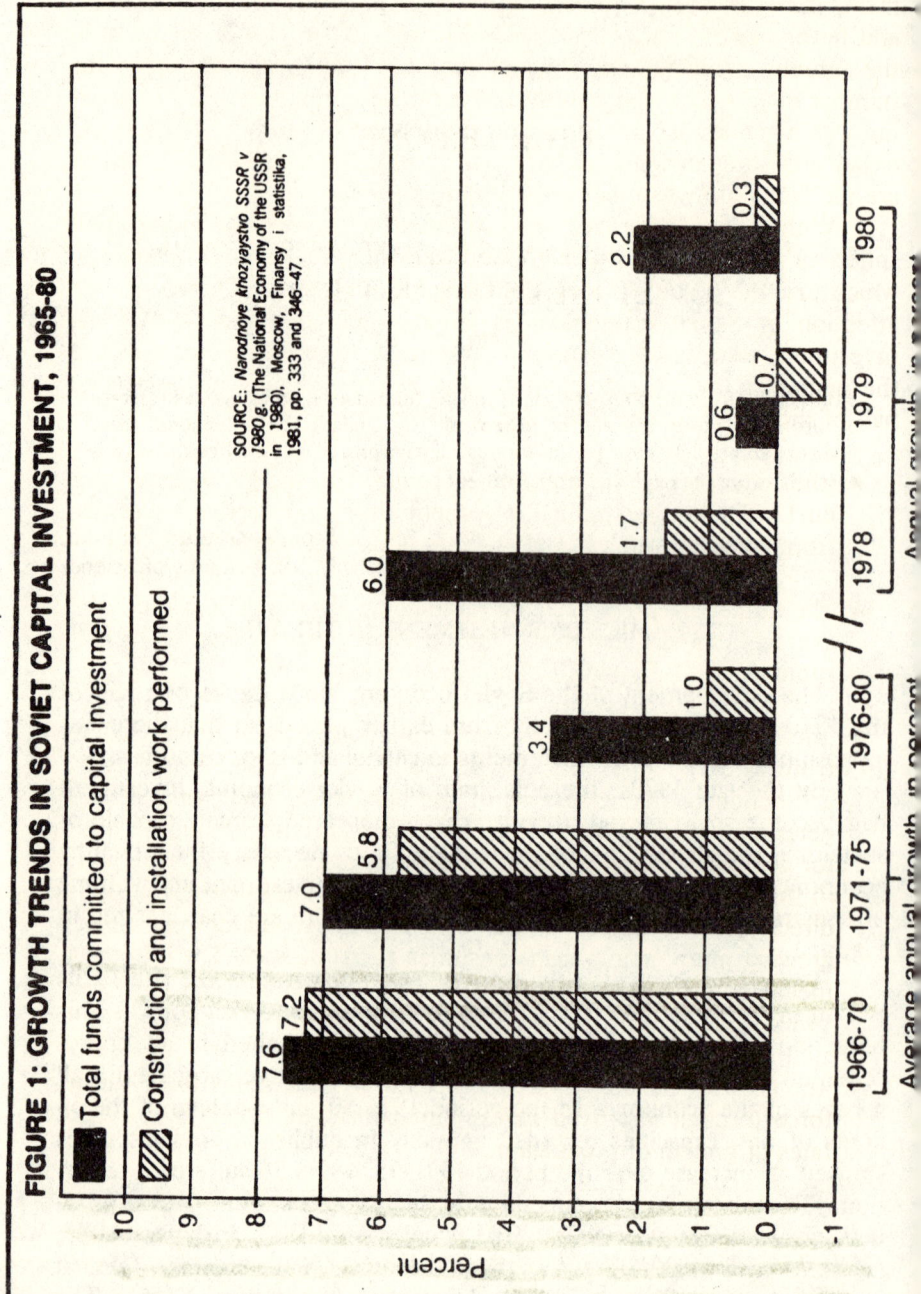

meat, milk, and sugar. There were fewer gas and oil pipelines built, and fewer railroad tracks and roads were laid. There was a reduction in the amount of drained and irrigated land put into use, as well as in the number of livestock and poultry farms put into operation. Less housing was made available. Moreover, production of many of these items either grew only insignificantly or was curtailed in the late 1970s.[1] Such are the fruits of investment activity in this period.

Within the framework of a planned economy, the investment sphere is much more subject to direct control than are labor resources, which are the result of long demographic processes. Therefore, the attention of Soviet economists is largely focused on improving the investment process at all stages. Among the factors that determined the nature of investment activity in the Soviet economy in the second half of the 1970s are the following:

- the reduction of the absolute increments to the gross social product. The average annual increment (in constant prices) declined from 46 billion rubles in 1971-75 to 40 billion rubles in 1976-80.[2]

- the reduction in the absolute increments to national income. The average annual increment (in constant prices) was 18 billion rubles in 1971-75 and 17 billion rubles in 1976-80.[3]

- the reduction of the share of accumulation in the national income from 29.5% in 1970 to 23.8% in 1980.[4] Such a trend is apparently a function of the realization of the dangers to the regime of any deterioration in the population's standard of living and of the need for economic incentives to stimulate labor productivity. However, in this regard it should be noted that, in contradiction to the Party directives, the output of the "means of production" has been growing more rapidly than consumer goods output. The output of means of production increased by 183 percent between 1970 and 1980, while consumer goods output increased by 165 percent.[5]

- the growing need to offset the decline in increments to the labor force through improved investment policies in order to maintain rates of growth of production.

[1] *Narkhoz 1980*, pp. 333, 346-347.
[2] *Narkhoz 1980*, pp. 328, 154, 158, 161-163, 165-173, 178-180.
[3] *Narkhoz 1980*, pp. 41-49.
[4] *Narkhoz 1980*, pp. 379-380.
[5] Loc cit.

- the continuing redistribution of capital investment in favor of agriculture and, thus, the decline in the share of other branches of the economy. The share of all forms of agriculture in total capital investment increased from 23.4 percent in 1966-70 to 27 percent in 1976-80.[6]

- the need to allocate growing investments just to maintain existing output levels in connection with the declining growth of the output of fuels and raw materials, which is in turn due to the reduced possibilities for expanding the raw material base and the insufficient scale of geological-prospecting work.

- the need for reducing the growing spatial disparity between the points of extraction of raw materials and fuel and their use. The amount of fuel transported from the east to European regions of the USSR increased from 130 million tons of standard fuel in 1970 to 360 in 1975. During this period the average length of haul for fuel increased by 22 percent, and total ton-kilometers of fuel shipments increased by 60 percent.[7]

Thus, on the one hand there is an obvious investment slump and a decline in the ability to invest, and on the other hand there is a growing need for a substantial increase in investment activity in order to slow the decline in the rate of economic growth.

CHARACTERISTICS OF THE INVESTMENT PROCESS

The distribution of capital investments within the national economy as a whole changed somewhat in the late '70s. At this level, the fundamental change was a diversion of funds from the so-called "nonproductive sphere" to agriculture, while the share of investment in the social sphere (home construction, trade, education, health care, etc.) dropped from 36 percent to 28 percent. Industry's share remained unchanged (a little more than 35 percent), and the share of transportation and communication grew somewhat. Within industrial investment, producers' goods started to receive a larger share at the expense of consumer goods.

In the investment dilemmas of the 1970s, the following factors were especially prominent.

---

[6] *Narkhoz 1980*, p. 124.
[7] *Narkhoz 1980*, p. 340.

First, as Figure 1 shows, there was a growing disproportion between the financial expression of investment and the physical resources needed to realize it. Second, there was a rise in the cost of all new productive capacities, even those having roughly the same structural and qualitative characteristics as those already in operation. According to the calculations of Vladimir Fal'tsman, one of the most competent specialists in Soviet investment practice, the average annual rate of this cost increase amounted to more than 6 percent in the latter half of the '70s, while in the same period the average annual growth rate of capital investment amounted to 3.4 per cent.[8] Apparently, the discrepancy between these two dynamic characteristics of the investment process is growing wider and wider. Presently, growing inflation in the area of investment is not taken into account in planning, statistics, or design. The inflation rate is almost double the rate of investment in the economy.

Third, the explosion of investments in the oil and gas industry which characterized this period as well as the growth of investments in agriculture, came at the expense of investments in metallurgy, machine-building, and construction materials. As a result, fewer productive capacities are being put into operation in these industries. The capacities that already exist are being utilized at a level which cannot be raised given the concrete conditions under which the Soviet economy is functioning. Therefore, we are starting to see an absolute drop in the production of metal, many kinds of machinery, and construction materials. The replacement of machinery and equipment is being curtailed, which means a drop in the technical level of production and a slower rate of automation. This, in turn, has slowed down technological progress throughout the economy as a whole, and is hindering the realization of the investment programs in agriculture and the oil-gas complex besides. Thus we can see that the new Soviet investment policy has boomeranged badly. Finally, there has been a lowering of investments in the consumer industries (i.e., light industry and food processing) and in the construction of housing, schools, stores, hospitals, nursuries, laundries, and other social programs. Investment in this so-called "non-productive" sphere dropped to 28 percent in the last five-year plan of the Brezhnev era (cf. 38 percent at the height of Krushchev's reign, 1955-60), and thus reached a record low for the whole Soviet postwar history.[9]

---

[8]Ia. Mazover, "Razmeshchenie toplivodobyvaiushchei promyshlennosti," *Planovoe khoziaistvo*, 1977, no. 11, pp. 137-149.

[9]V. Fal'tsman, "Moshchnostnoi ekvivalent osnovnykh fondov," *Voprosy ekonomiki*, no. 8, 1980.

THE DYNAMICS OF THE CAPITAL COEFFICIENT

Under these conditions the Soviet rulers were forced to reexamine both theoretical and practical approaches to economic growth. With the declining growth rates of basic factors of production, increased attention has been given to increasing the efficiency of their use. Soviet economists have created the concept of a special, *intensive*, type of expanded reproduction under the conditions of "developed socialism," which differs from the *extensive* type that is characteristic of socialism per se. In attempting to reflect reality, contemporary Soviet economic theory explains that the need for intensifying the reproduction process under conditions of "developed socialism" is due to the fact that the possibilities for economic development based on "extensive" factors, which previously resulted in high growth rates, are now exhausted. It follows from this that the only way to avoid a slowing of economic development is to increase the return on capital and labor.

However, in point of fact the return on both capital and on labor declined during the second half of the 1970s in comparison with the first half of the decade. The increment in national income per ruble of capital investment for the economy as a whole in constant prices was 28 percent lower during 1976-80 than during 1971-1975.[10] The average annual increment to produced national income per employee in material production (in constant prices) declined by approximately 10 percent during this period.[11]

Facing very limited possibilities due to the demographic situation for managing the economy by manipulating labor resources (more than 90 percent of the able-bodied population is employed), Soviet economic managers to a large degree have concentrated their efforts in the investment sphere. The increase in the intensiveness of production must be attained through a growth in labor productivity by supplying the labor force with ever more sophisticated and effective fixed assets. This means that the rate of growth of labor productivity must be greater than the growth of the capital/labor ratio. And this in turn implies an increase in the output/capital ratio. The intensification of production must be manifested in an increase in the return on capital or a reduction in the capital coefficient (capital/output ratio).

---

[10] *Narkhoz 1980*, pp. 333, 379; *Narkhoz 1980*, p. 563; *Vestnik statistiki*, 1980, no. 4, p. 68.
[11] *Narkhoz 1980*, p. 379; *Narkhoz 1975*, p. 563; *Vestnik statistiki*, 1980, no. 4, p. 68. Aggregate labor productivity was calculated according to the methodology of the USSR Central Statistical Administration as defined in *Narkhoz 1978*, p. 575. The number employed in material production was calculated from data given in *Narkhoz 1980*, pp. 355, 357.

In fact just the opposite phenomenon is observed in the Soviet economy the output/capital ratio is steadily falling both in the economy as a whole and in all of its branches. The decline in this ratio in Soviet industry is a trend that began at the end of the 1950s. However, in the second half of the 1970s it took on new scope. The output/capital ratio in industry, calculated as the increment in gross output per ruble of capital investment in industry (both in constant prices), with no lag considered, declined from 0.88 rubles in 1971-75 to 0.53 rubles in 1976-80,[12] or by 40 percent.

It is possible that the decline in the output/capital ratio might have been compensated by a reduction in current production expenditures. But the facts refute this suggestion: the recoupment period of capital investment in industry increased from 5 to 11 years during 1960-75 and it increased still further to 25 years by 1977, when it was three times greater than the established norm.[13]

Nor can this trend in the output/capital ratio and the sharp jump in the investment recoupment period be explained by changes in the branch structure of industry. The share of branches with relatively low output/capital ratios has tended to decline, and there is no trend toward an increase in the share of branches with a relatively high ratio of current production expenditures to gross output.

The shift of extractive industry to the east also does not explain this phenomenon. The share of Siberia and the Far East in total national capital investment has remained practically stable over a period of many years at the level of about 15-16 percent.[14] Furthermore, the negative effects of the shift of industry to eastern regions on the output/capital ratio should in general not be exaggerated. Although the greater demands of the climate and other natural conditions are often emphasized, some favorable conditions in the east must also be taken into account—the larger coal seams in the coal industry, the richer ores in nonferrous metallurgy, and the better quality of timber in the lumber industry.[15]

---

[12] *Narkhoz 1980*, p. 336; *Vestnik statistiki*, 1980, no. 4, p. 68; *Narkhoz 1975*, p. 191; *Narkhoz 1980*, p. 123. Capital investment in industry in 1979 was determined using the average share of industry in total capital investment in the economy during 1975-80—35 percent.

[13] T. Khachaturov, "Puti povysheniia effektivnosti kapital'nykh vlozhenii," *Voprosy ekonomiki*, 1979, no. 7, p. 124.

[14] V. Krasovskii, "Ekonomicheskie problemy fondootdachi," *Voprosy ekonomiki*, 1980, no. 1, p. 108.

[15] A. Aganbegian, "Ekonomicheskie problemy razvitiia Sibiri," *Ekonomika i matematicheskie metody*, vol. XV, 1979, vypusk 5, pp. 843-844.

There is a growing discussion in the Soviet economic literature about increasing ecological expenditures as a factor that is making new production capacity more expensive. However, this factor does not have a very significant effect on the capital intensiveness of production. Its share in the over all increase in the capital/output ratio in ferrous metallurgy, for example, is no more than 10-11 percent.[16]

The output/capital ratio depends to a certain extent on fluctuations in the utilization of productive capacities that were put into operation earlier and that have no relation to investments made during the period being considered. This is especially significant in the Soviet economy since bringing new production capacity to full utilization in some instances can take years. This phenomenon is of particular importance during the period of extensive reconstruction of an industrial enterprise. It is not possible with available statistics to determine an output/capital ratio for industry as a whole or for its individual branches that is free of the distorting influence of this factor. However, data on the utilization of basic types of equipment in several branches of industry (electrical power, ferrous metallurgy, and cement)[17] over a number of years do not reflect any deterioration in the utilization of productive capacities. It is unlikely that this is a factor underlying the decline in the output/capital ratio. Judging from these data and from trends in indicators reflecting the average number of shifts worked, the level of utilization of existing capacities has not changed substantially over time.

Thus, the share of newly activated fixed capital is declining, and the productivity of assets put into operation earlier is not showing any tendency to decline but has rather remained more or less stable. The decline in the output/capital ratio therefore can be explained only by an accelerating decline in the productivity of new assets.

BASIC FACTORS WHICH RAISE THE CAPITAL COEFFICIENT

Two basic factors are inherent in the investment process in the USSR a growth in the cost of new technology and equipment that is more rapid than the increase in its productivity, and an imbalance between the number of projects under construction and the material resources for carrying out this extensive construction program.

With respect to the first factor, there is a special directive in the "Basic Directions for the Development of the National Economy of the USSR during 1976-1980" adopted by the 25th Party Congress: "The

---

[16] P. Shiriaev and V. Shtanskii, *Effektivnost' kapitalnykh vlozhenii v chernoi metallurgii*, Moscow: Metallurgiia, 1977, p. 188.
[17] *Narkhoz 1978*, p. 139.

most important requirement in developing new designs of machines, instruments, and apparatus must be to achieve the maximum economic effect while *reducing their cost per unit of capacity*" (my emphasis).[18] The wholesale price indexes that are published and used in Soviet statistics on industrial output, including those for branches that produce fixed assets (the investment branches), show a favorable trend. The overall wholesale price index for all industry in 1978, with 1949=100, was 63. The corresponding indexes for the investment branches were 33 in machine building and metalworking and 67 in construction materials. The price index rose only in the fuels and wood products branches.[19] At the same time, the price index for the actual cost of construction-installation work also declined.[20]

However, even in the opinion of some Soviet economists these data are not considered reliable. The price indexes are compiled on the basis of a narrow group of goods that are not representative of the entire volume of capital investment, and reductions in price are not common for the majority of new assets. Quite the contrary, investment output is characterized by an exceptionally high rate of price increases. It is precisely in branches of the investment complex (machine building and construction materials) that a sharp and continuing increase in prices is taking place. In the authoritative opinion of V. Krasovskii, the source of price pressures in the Soviet economy is not fuel and raw materials prices but "... the most unregulated and uncontrolled change in prices in branches of the construction industry and investment machine-building."[21]

The cost of the components of fixed capital—construction output and equipment—has increased steadily for many years (at least since the beginning of the 1960s), and this increase has been especially significant during the 1970s. The results of a study of trends in the prices of investment goods conducted by the USSR Stroibank showed that the increase was not less than 10 percent during 1971-75.[22] A single example that illustrates the scale of the phenomenon is that capital expenditures on the production of one ton of steel increased from 431.3 rubles during 1965-70 to 586.1 rubles in 1971-75 and to 760.5 rubles in 1976-1980.[23]

---

[18] *KPSS v rezoliutsiiakh i resheniiakh s"ezdov, konferentsii i plenumov TsK*, vol. XII, 1975-77, Moscow: Politicheskaia literatura, 1978, pp. 200-201.
[19] *Narkhoz 1978*, p. 139.
[20] Ibid., p. 360.
[21] Krasovskii, "Ekonomicheskie," 1980, p. 109.
[22] Ibid., p. 110.
[23] Shiriaev and Shtanskii, *Effektivnost'*, 1977, p. 188.

Numerous data published in the Soviet press attest to the sharp increase in the cost per unit of capacity of equipment put into operation during the 1970s. Most common is the growth of the size and weight of equipment per unit of productive capacity. Thus, the conclusion may be drawn that there is a capital-using trend in the development of technology and equipment in Soviet industry, in which the growth in unit productive capacity has been exceeded by growing expenditures of resources.

The second continuing factor—the imbalance between the number of construction projects and the resources necessary to carry them out—is also a chronic phenomenon that intensified during the second half of the 1970s. While the rates of growth and the absolute increments to capital investment were declining, the overall estimated cost of newly begun industrial construction almost doubled in the period 1976-79 as compared with 1971-75.[24] As a result the cost of all projects under construction was 8-9 times greater than the annual value of capital investment. This process is accelerating—the annual average value of uncompleted construction on productive projects increased by 34 percent between 1971-75 and 1976-80.[25]

THE DEVELOPMENT OF THE CONSTRUCTION SECTOR OF THE ECONOMY

A description of the current state of the investment sphere in the USSR would be incomplete without a look at economic indicators for the construction sector itself. The slowing of growth rates and decline in absolute increments that took place in the Soviet economy during the second half of the 1970s applies to this sector as well.

In the late 1970s (1978-80) the volume of construction work ceased to grow entirely, and even showed a slight trend towards decline.[26] The growth rate of labor productivity in the construction industry dropped from 29 percent in the first half of the '70s to 11 percent in the second half.[27]

At the same time there has been a reduction the increments to employment the increment of workers in the construction industry dropped 200 percent in the second half of the 1970s as compared to the first half.[28]

---

[24]V. Kirichenko, "Intensifikatsiia i sbalansirovannost' ekonomicheskogo rosta," *Planovoe khoziaistvo*, 1979, no. 2, p. 47.
[25]*Narkhoz 1980*, p. 345.
[26]See *Narkhoz 1980*, pp. 346-347.
[27]*Narkhoz 1980*, p. 351.
[28]Ibid.

Given the trends noted, there should have been an increase in the average amount of equipment per construction worker. However, while fixed capital in construction increased during the second half of the 1970s, the increases in the amount of construction equipment were smaller. During the periods 1966-70, 1971-75, and 1976-80, respectively, the average annual increases in the numbers of certain basic types of construction equipment were as follows: (in thousands): excavators—6.8, 7.4, and 4.8; scrapers—1.8, 2.4, and 0.5; and bulldozers—6.6, 8.0, and 4.0. Only in the number of movable cranes was there a slight increase: 7.1, 9.6, and 10.0.[29]

It is improbable that during 1971-80 there was a significant increase in the unit productivity of construction equipment leading to a reduction in the number of machines needed. The contradiction between the continuing growth of the value of fixed capital in the construction industry (average annual growth rates of 13 percent in 1966-70, 10 percent in 1971-75, and 9 percent in 1976-80) and the decline in the growth of the number of basic types of machines is very likely due to a sharp increase in prices of construction machinery that is not reflected in the Soviet price indexes.[30] This leads to the conclusion that the amount of fixed assets per ruble of construction output is much lower in physical terms than in value terms.

The average current production costs in construction work, which decreased during 1971-75, showed a tendency to increase during the second half of the 1970s. Consequently, the growth of productive capacities in the construction industry was reduced in the second half of the 1970s, and construction became more expensive.

Thus, not only did investment activity slow down in the last decade; the development of the construction industry's potential also virtually ground to a halt.

---

[29] *Narkhoz 1980*, p. 350.
[30] *Narkhoz 1980*, p. 49; D. Palterovich, *Park proizvodstvennogo oborudovaniia*, Moscow: Nauka, 1970, p. 192.

CHAPTER TWO

RENOVATION VERSUS CONSTRUCTION: THE FOCUS OF INDUSTRIAL INVESTMENT POLICY

> Allow me to voice one general consideration which is directly connected with the fate of old plants. As soon as we get down to renovation, we run up against the fact that the outlines of the technological program in the industry and at individual enterprises have been oriented in advance towards continuous galvanization of the old technology. Fifteen to twenty years in advance, we create the kind of situation in which the only thing we can do is patch old clothes, instead of making ourselves new ones.
>
> Prof. A. A. Fedotov, Moscow Institute
> of Steel and Alloys, 1978

PRIORITY INVESTMENT IN THE RENOVATION OF EXISTING ENTERPRISES

The key idea of investment policy in the 1970s became to limit capital investment in the creation of new industrial enterprises and to redirect investment resources to increase productive capacities through the renovation, expansion, and modernization of existing ones. The path of "reconstruction"[1] has been labeled in state and party documents as one of the main directions of economic policy, and it has become the object of a propaganda campaign. The voices of economists opposed to this all-encompassing emphasis on reconstruction, who call for seeking optimal proportions in the distribution of capital investments between the construction of new and the renovation of existing enterprises, are drowned out by the united proponents of "reconstruction" who see in it a clear advantage.

The scale of reconstruction has taken on such dimensions and the share of investment directed to it has become so great (almost three-fourths of all industrial capital investment), that it is fair to say that reconstruction has a decisive influence on the structure of investment and fixed capital, on the rate of turnover of capital expenditures, and on the pace and nature of technological progress in industry.

---

[1] Here and below, unless otherwise specified, the term "reconstruction" is used to refer to any form of renovating and expanding an existing enterprise. A more precise definition is given below.

The central planning bureaucracy has been rooting objects of new construction out of the projected plans of branch ministries, and switching resources over to the renovation and expansion of already existing enterprises. As a result, the percentage industrial investments earmarked for the renovation and expansion of older enterprises has increased from 58 to 72 percent between 1970 and 1980. The share of reconstruction in capital investments in individual branches of industry increased by the following amounts between 1970 and 1980 (in percent):[2]

- electric and thermal power, from 20 to 34;
- ferrous metallurgy, from 60 to 80;
- chemical and petrochemical industry, from 45 to 66;
- machine building and metalworking, from 63 to 80;
- wood and paper industry, from 57 to 75;
- construction materials industry, from 50 to 74;
- light industry, from 40 to 75; and
- food industry, from 66 to 80.

Only in the coal industry was there a reduction in the share of reconstruction due to the development of new coal deposits in eastern regions (the Kansk-Achinsk and others). It should also be taken into account that in the preceding decade the share of reconstruction in capital investment in all of these branches except construction materials either declined or remained stable.

The sharp increase in the number of industrial enterprises undergoing reconstruction led to a significant increase in their size. While the number of industrial enterprises increased very little between 1960 and 1975, the value of fixed capital per enterprise increased steadily and rapidly—from 3.5 million rubles in the mid-1960s to more than eight million rubles in 1975.[3]

Although the stated goal of reconstruction is to reduce aggregate (capital and labor) expenses, the real concern of the economic leadership is to achieve output increases through reconstruction, which is supposed to require lower relative capital expenditures than does new construction.

[2] *Narkhoz 1975*, p. 509; *Narkhoz 1980*, p. 339.
[3] TsU SSSR, *Promyshlennost' SSSR: statisticheskii sbornik*, Moscow: Statistika, 1964, p. 82; *Narkhoz 1975*, p. 189.

WHAT GOSPLAN MEANS BY "RECONSTRUCTION," AND WHAT ACTUALLY HAPPENS

Before turning to an examination of the results of this policy, it is necessary to define "reconstruction." In this text, as in the Soviet literature, this term is used in the broad sense, combining all forms of rebuilding and expanding existing enterprises. However, in Soviet planning and design, and in statistical accounts, three forms of developing existing enterprises are distinguished as alternatives to new construction: expansion (*rasshirenie*), reconstruction (*rekonstruktsiia*), and retooling (*tekhnicheskoe perevooryzhenie*).

In 1975 Gosplan and Gosstroy published[4] the following definitions of these three forms in an attempt to encompass and regulate all the various types of work on rebuilding existing enterprises.

Expansion: The construction of second and later phases of existing enterprises on the basis of a new design, and also the expansion of existing basic production shops simultaneously with the expansion (increase in carrying capacity) of auxiliary and service facilities and communications. At the same time the technological level of the entire enterprise is raised and its economic operating indicators are improved.

Reconstruction: The complete or partial replacement of equipment and/or rebuilding of facilities without constructing new basic production shops or expanding existing ones. Reconstruction may be accompanied by the expansion and even new construction of auxiliary and service facilities. It should involve the replacement of old equipment, the mechanization and automation of production, and the elimination of "bottlenecks." Reconstruction also includes the construction of new shops and facilities to replace those being liquidated when the old and new facilities are of the same capacity.

Retooling: Measures to raise the technical level of production without expanding the size of the enterprise. "Passive" components of fixed capital—buildings and structures—are essentially left untouched, but equipment is modernized, old machines are replaced with new ones, and new technology is introduced, i.e., primarily the "active" components of fixed capital are updated.

What are the essential ideas in these definitions? The definition of "reconstruction" per se excludes the construction of new or expansion of existing shops and basic production facilities, except to replace equal capacities being liquidated. This requirement makes the definition of reconstruction itself devoid of any practical meaning.

---

[4]"Instruktivnoe pis'mo Gosplana SSSR i Gosstroiia ot 6 Fevralia 1975 g," no. VI-4-D-10-D, *Biulleten' normativnykh aktov ministerstv i vedomstv SSSR*, 1975, no. 5, pp. 47, 48.

The definition of expansion is much more realistic. It is convenient because it erodes the boundary between expansion as such and the construction of actual new enterprises on sites adjoining existing facilities. This makes it possible to avoid the strict limitations placed on new construction, and branch and enterprise managers are taking advantage of this possibility to create new production facilities under the stamp of "expansion." A condition that must be observed in doing this is that the newly created facilities must be spatially linked to the existing plant. However, nowhere—in none of the methodic or normative guidelines—is there any mention of permissible limits on the distance between the sites of the old and new facilities. They may be directly adjacent to each other or they may be separated by several miles, as was the case in the pseudo-expansion of the Zdolbunovskii and Katav-Ivanov cement plants, blast-furnace N° 9 of the Krivoi-Rog metallurgical plant, the Leninskii Komsomol automobile plant in Moscow, and many other enterprises.

Thus, a sort of hybrid has been developed from new construction and reconstruction. The latter introduces an emphasis on augmenting the production capacities of industrial complexes that are already operating using infrastructure and raw materials supplies that are largely already in place, as well as the rebuilding of old facilities. But at the same time new facilities are also attached; new buildings, structures, and communications facilities are constructed based on new designs.

The restructuring of enterprises under the definition of "reconstruction" and "retooling" accounts for an insignificant share of total capital investment in existing facilities. Most of this total is allocated for "expansion." But this fact cannot be established from published statistical information since only data on the overall total for "reconstruction, expansion, and retooling of existing enterprises" is reported in the statistical handbooks issued by the Central Statistical Administration. Nonetheless, some fragmentary evidence gives an impression of the extent of reconstruction per se that does not involve the construction of new productive facilities. For example, in 1974, of the total amount of capital investment in the reconstruction of existing industrial enterprises in Belorussia, only 15 percent did not involve the construction of new facilities.[5] But it is precisely this form of reconstruction that is most effective from the standpoint of the established aims of this policy.

---

[5]P. Kapitula et al., *Fondoemkost' obshchestvennogo proizvodstva*, Minsk: Nauka i tekhnika, 1977, pp. 78-79.

In economic circles there is an effort to disguise the fact that, in spite of state and party directives, true reconstruction is taking place in insignificant amounts. The predominant trend is toward a much more resource-intensive form of increasing capacity—new construction, spatially linked to existing enterprises and undertaken under the rubric of reconstruction and expansion.

Sometimes conflicting information appears, which reveals the true state of affairs. According to data of the Central Statistical Administration, the share of capital investment in reconstruction, expansion, and retooling of existing enterprises in ferrous metallurgy increased from 60 to 80 percent between 1970 and 1980.[6] At the same time one of the directors of the state institute for the design of metallurgical plants, P. Shiriaev, stated that "... about 7 percent is directed toward reconstruction and 93 percent to new construction"[7] (the reference is to the same period). The explanation for this contradiction is that the basic approach to increasing production capacity in ferrous metallurgy during the 1970s was the construction of new shops and production lines on sites adjoining existing plants. Plant designer Shiriaev, using technical-economic design estimates, considers this type of investment as "new construction," while at the same time branch directors include it in planning and statistical materials as "reconstruction and expansion."

Substituting concepts leads to a substitution of meaning. This form of reconstruction is transformed from a means of economizing on investment resources to a very expensive form of increasing capacities.

A study of the effectiveness of capital investments in metallurgical plants during 1966-80 done by the Central Economic Scientific Research Institute of the RSFSR Gosplan showed that capital investments per ton of increase in output at new plants were about 55 percent of those for the reconstruction and expansion of existing enterprises.[8] The authors of this study reached the conclusion that the branch had gone beyond the limits of economic effectiveness of the reconstruction and expansion of existing plants. Nonetheless, this form of increasing production capacities was included in all planning variants for the 1980s.

Branch directors, enterprise managers, planners, and designers who think sensibly realize that there are only negligible gains to be realized from the forms of resource-saving renovation defined under the headings "reconstruction" and "retooling." In some branches of industry there are no gains to be made. But it is important to branch

---

[6] *Narkhoz 1980*, p. 339, *Narkhoz 1970*, p. 485.
[7] *Metodika i praktika opredeleniia effektivnosti kapital'nykh vlozhenii i novoi tekhniki*, no. 28, Moscow: Nauka, 1976, p. 49.
[8] Ibid., no. 26, 1976, p. 119.

directors and enterprise managers to include any variant of capital construction in the plan to attain an increase in productive capacity and to prove to Gosplan that allocate capital investment and regulate its use that the variants proposed are the most economical and (of most importance) the least capital intensive. If there is a high-level directive to allocate capital investments primarily for reconstruction, then the proposals of branch and enterprise managers will be for reconstruction, even if in fact what is happening is the construction of a new enterprise adjoining an old one.

THE GOALS OF RENOVATION AND THEIR REALIZATION

In order to understand the essence of the reconstruction of industry that is taking place in the USSR, it is necessary to examine the quantitative and qualitative aspects of how the physical plant of enterprises undergoing reconstruction is being updated within the framework of the basic aims that have been stated:

- Updating must involve primarily the replacement of equipment and only to minimal extent buildings and structures. It follows that the share of construction-installation work in total investment and the share of buildings and structures in total fixed capital must be significantly reduced. The share of equipment must increase correspondingly.

- Equipment that is retired must be replaced by equipment that is more modern. It must make possible a reduction in current production expenditures and, thus, shorten the recoupment time of capital expenditures.

- The period between the time when capital expenditures are made and when output increases begin must be shortened.

Let us now consider how this triune goal was realized over the past ten years, and how beneficial was the effect of renovation investment policy on the results of investment activity in Soviet industry. Please note that here we do not mean to explain the dynamics of various indicators exclusively through the influence of this factor. In every case this is the result of innumerable contrary forces. But for all of that, a change in the investment flow in the direction of already existing enterprises, such as occurred in the '70s, could not help but render a dominant influence on the functioning of the whole industrial investment sphere; furthermore, it could not but decisively affect (directly or indirectly) the economics of industrial production as a whole, including the dynamics of production expenses.

MAXIMUM INVESTMENT IN EQUIPMENT, MINIMUM INVESTMENT IN BUILDINGS AND STRUCTURE

Data characterizing the trend in the technical structure[9] of capital investment are contradictory. According to official Soviet data reported in CEMA statistical handbooks the share of equipment is rising,[10] but according to figures cited by some authors it is falling.[11] Price trends differ for construction output and machine-building production, and this is a significant factor underlying changes over time in the technical structure of capital investment. A comparative analysis of these price trends for different components of investment would require a great deal of information and a separate detailed study, which is beyond the scope of this work. Therefore, our discussion will focus on one of the most authoritative scholars in this area, V. Fal'tsman, who carried out a study of changes in the technical structure of capital investment in the major branches of industry at the Central Mathematical-Economics Institute of the USSR Academy of Sciences. Comparing the trends of change in the share of capital expenditures on equipment and the share of reconstruction in capital investment for 1966-70 and 1971-75, he writes:

> The growth of the share of expenditures on equipment in capital investment is usually associated with a change in the reproductive structure of investment—an increase in the share of reconstruction. However, analysis of changes in the reproductive structure for individual branches of industry reveals a different situation.[12]

Fal'tsman notes further that in all branches except machine building the share of expenditures on reconstruction, expansion, and retooling grew substantially. At the same time the share of expenditures on equipment declined in four branches (ferrous metallurgy, machine building, light industry, and food industry), and in all other branches this share either remained stable or increased negligibly.

---

[9]In Soviet economic terminology the "technical structure" means the division of capital investment into expenditures on construction-installation work and on equipment, and the division of fixed capital into "passive" components (buildings and structures) and "active" components (equipment).

[10]See, for example, Sovet ekonomicheskoi vzaimopomoshchi, *Statisticheskii ezhegodnik stran-chlenov soveta ekonomicheskoi vzaimopomoshchi: 1979*, Moscow: Statistika, 1979, pp. 184-207.

[11]V. Fal'tsman, A Ozhegov, "Proportsii v razvitii mashinostroeniia i stroitel'stva," *Izvestiya Akademii nauk SSSR, Seriya ekonomicheskaya*, 1981, no. 2, pp. 67-69. N. Podshivalenko, "Puti sokrashcheniia stoimosti stroitel'stva," *Voprosy ekonomiki*, 1981, no. 1, p. 28.

[12]V. Fal'tsman, "Intensifikatsiia razvitiia proizvodstvennogo apparata," *Voprosy ekonomiki*, 1978, no. 1, p. 34.

The increase in the share of construction-installation work corresponds to the trend in the share of so-called "passive" components (buildings and structures) of fixed capital in industry. During the 1950 to 1980 period, the latter fell from 51 to 48 percent in current prices.[13] The decline in the share of passive components of fixed capital is explained by the drop in the share of structures (*sooruzhenie*)—from 21 to 19 percent during 1970-78. There was almost no decline in the share of buildings, which is a major objective of reconstruction efforts. This share was 28 percent in 1950 and 28.9 percent in 1980.[14]

It might be suggested that price factors influence the technical structure of fixed capital—that the change in the shares of active and passive components were distorted by differing trends in the prices of machine building and construction output. There certainly are indications in the specialist literature to the effect that the growth of prices of machinery has been substantially greater than the increase in the cost of construction output, and the share of equipment in fixed capital has, accordingly, increased. According to estimates of D. Palterovich[15] and V. Krasovskii,[16] the annual growth of the cost of equipment due to price increases in the 1960s was 2-2.5 percent. Judging from more recent literature the growth of prices on machine-building products has not slowed.[17] Consequently, if the effect of the price factor on the growth of the share of active components of fixed capital were eliminated trends in the technical structure would appear even less favorable.

Thus, the growing predominance of reconstruction in investment programs is not leading to an improvement in the techical structure of capital investment and fixed capital. Let us examine the reasons for this tendency.

First of all, do changes in the branch structure have an effect? An analysis showed that this factor does not influence the trend in overall indicators for industry of the technical structure of fixed capital.[18] Two factors hinder the reduction of the share of construction-installation work in capital expenditures and the share of "passive" components of fixed capital in Soviet industry. First, the growth in the size of equipment and the scale of equipment assemblies. The increase

[13]TsSU SSSR, *Promyshlennost' SSSR: Statisticheskii sbornik*, Moscow: Gosstatizdat, 1957, p. 16; *Narkhoz 1980*, p. 143.
[14]Ibid.
[15]Palterovich, *Park*, 1970, p. 198.
[16]V. Krasovskii, *Intensifikatsiia i rezervy ekonomiki*, Moscow: Nauka, 1970, p. 279.
[17]V. Fal'tsman and I. Zasorina, "Fondootdacha i kapitaloemkost' toplivnoenergeticheskogo kompleksa," *Voprosy ekonomiki*, 1979, no. 3, pp. 28-29.
[18]*Narkhoz 1975*, p. 223; *Narkhoz 1980*, p. 143.

in the concentration of industrial production in the USSR has taken place as a result of the growth of the so-called "unit concentration" (*agregatnoy kontsentratsii*)—the increase of production capacities of equipment and assemblies—which is achieved in most branches of industry by introducing equipment of a much larger scale. This phenomenon is particularly apparent in branches of industry with a technology based on the use of large complexes of equipment such as metallurgy, chemicals, petrochemicals, construction materials, etc. According to estimates made by Ia. Kvasha,[19] the concentration of capacity of equipment complexes increased an average annual rate of 5 percent during the 1960s. This process continued during the 1970s.

Second, the complexity and, thus, the cost of construction-installation work in building over larger equipment complexes is further increased when work is done within existing enterprises. The structure of construction-installation work itself has not remained stable. The share of installation work decreased by 13 percent in 1971-75 in comparison with the previous five-year period.[20] The share of construction work proper increased accordingly. Installation work is to a large extent associated with setting up equipment and equipment complexes.

We may note, incidentally, that the practice in Soviet statistics of including installation work in construction output is not very appropriate. An increase in the share of capital expenditures on construction as the share of reconstruction rises contradicts the desired direction of change in the technological structure of investment and increases capital expenditures per unit increase of capacity attained by reconstruction. The increase in expenditures on construction is explained by the need for a radical rather than partial (as planned) renovation of passive components of fixed capital in the course of reconstruction. This renovation takes place in two directions.

- First is the construction of new buildings and structures during the course of reconstruction.

- Second is the huge amount of work on the repair, alteration, and modernization of industrial facilities that is growing with the increase in the volume of reconstruction work and that is to a significant extent unplanned, unregulated, and poorly reflected in Soviet statistical accounts. The scale of this phenomenon was revealed at the time of the general inventory of fixed capital in 1972. It was determined then that when buildings and structures

---

[19]Ia. B. Kvasha, *Reservnye moshchnosti*, Moscow: Nauka, 1971, pp. 166-67.
[20]Fal'tsman, "Intensifikatsiia," 1978, p. 27.

were rebuilt and machinery and equipment reinstalled during the reconstruction of enterprises (the expansion of buildings, increasing their height, replacing crane supports, etc.) the parts razed were in many cases not written off since the assets continued to be formally carried on the books. The general inventory discovered billions of rubles of this sort of capital expenditures not written off.[21]

WHY THE RECONSTRUCTION OF OLD BUILDINGS AND THE CONSTRUCTION OF NEW BUILDINGS HAVE BECOME SO WIDESPREAD IN THE COURSE OF RENOVATION

The increase in the extent of renovation of the passive components of fixed capital, which was unavoidable given the massive reconstruction of enterprises during the 1970s, is explained by a peculiarity of the investment process in Soviet industry. This is that in spite of the high rates of growth and thus the extensive updating and renovation of fixed capital the deterioration of passive components worsened.

The retirement and scrappage of passive components due to physical wear and tear, judging from available statistics, did not exceed 0.5-0.8 percent of their average annual value during the 1970s.[22] Even in the mid-1930s when about 50 percent of industrial capital investment went for the construction of new enterprises,[23] the share of old production buildings constructed before the revolution was about 60 percent, and the share built in the previous century was 30 percent.[24] Furthermore, it should be taken into account that the replacement value of industrial fixed capital declined by 7 percent during the years of the revolution and the civil war.[25]

The effort to limit capital expenditures on buildings and structures as much as possible was always a characteristic feature of Soviet investment policy and always took an extreme form. It was reflected even in definitions and terminology: in the early 1930s the terms "unproductive capital" (*neproduktivnyi kapital*) and "productive capital" (*produktivnyi kapital*) were used for buildings and structures and for equipment, respectively.[26] Subsequently they were transformed into "passive" and

---

[21] Ia. Kvasha, "Tekhnicheskii progress, sroki sluzhby sredstv truda i otraslevaia struktura," in *Proportsii vosproizvodstva v period razvitogo sotsializma*, Moscow: Nauka, 1976, p. 122.
[22] *Narkhoz 1975*, p. 225; *Narkhoz 1980*, p. 147.
[23] A. Notkin, *Ocherki teorii sotsialisticheskogo vosproizvodstva*, Moscow: Gospolitizdat, 1948, p. 202.
[24] Ia. Kvasha, *Amortizatsiia i sroki sluzhby osnovnykh fondov*, Moscow: Izdatel'stvo AN SSSR, 1959, p. 136.
[25] M. Barun, *Osnovnoi kapital promyshlennosti SSSR*, Moscow: Gosizdat, 1930, p. 36.
[26] Ibid., p. 59.

"active" fixed capital. These very designations indicate the need to reduce nonproductive, passive capital in any way possible. No effort is even made to determine the optimal correlation between the passive and active components, which naturally cannot be the same in all climatic zones and in production facilities with different technologies. Only capital investments that achieve a minimum share of expenditures on passive components (in comparison with previous designs) are considered efficient.

Such a policy pursued over a period of 60 years yields its results; the striving for maximum savings on buildings and structures in constructing new industrial facilities led later to excessive expenditures on their repair, reconstruction, and modernization, which grew especially rapidly during the 1970s in connection with the massive reconstruction of enterprises.

The rebuilding, expansion, and modernization of buildings during reconstruction is not only carried out on the basis of capital spending but also consumes depreciation allowances for capital repair. In 1976 expenditures on capital repair in industry were 144 percent of depreciation allowances for this purpose, and in a number of branches this ratio exceeded 200 percent. At the same time depreciation allowances for capital repair of equipment were underutilized by 18.4 percent.[27]

In addition to physical wear and tear, there are other quite natural reasons for rebuilding industrial buildings and structures, especially the need for modernization in the light of technological progress. The development of such branches of industry as radiotechnical, electronic, precision machine-building, instrument building and others has resulted in a sharp increase in the demands made on industrial buildings by the design and engineering of equipment, and these demands are growing rapidly. In old buildings, due to the technological requirements of a whole series of production processes, it became impossible to produce many types of products with sufficient precision and reliability. The comprehensive mechanization and automation of production processes and the introduction of assembly-line methods in the process of reconstruction required changing the very principles of the overall layout of industrial buildings. The need for increasing productivity and improving working conditions resulted in a change in the technical characteristics of buildings—improved lighting of workplaces, ventilation, etc. All of this together sharply increased the role of passive components of fixed capital in carrying out the reconstruction of facilities.

[27]M. Zavalishin and A. Masal'skii, "Novye normy amortizatsii: itogi i problemy," *Planovoe khoziaistvo*, 1978, no. 5, p. 69.

As a result of the strict limitations on investment in the rebuilding of passive components of fixed capital, construction work undertaken during reconstruction does not fundamentally solve the problem and lays the foundation for still more expensive future reconstruction. Reconstruction projects at enterprises follow one after another, and it would be natural to carry out the reconstruction of passive components not only from the standpoint of current needs. The construction of any sort of addition or "mini-building" makes it possible to install new equipment immediately. But each subsequent stage of reconstruction turns out to be more and more expensive and difficult since continually locating new buildings at the same enterprise and rebuilding existing ones becomes more complex, and the scheme of technological links and transport sites becomes more and more confused. The next alteration of buildings, structures, and pipelines requires even more additional investments.

The only solution that might radically change the situation in the future at many enterprises undergoing reconstruction and which apparently could be realized (it has already been implemented in recent years in priority branches of industry such as instrument building, radiotechnical industry, and others) is the construction of prefabricated buildings at large enterprises. The construction of prefabricated buildings, in turn, involves solving some extremely complex questions. One problem that arises is that of siting the new building, which must be drawn in to the overall technological scheme of the enterprise. A new building requires space that, near the primary production shops, may be heavily used by communication lines, power facilities, and other supporting structures. Thus, the construction of such shops is possible only with the radical restructuring of the main technological part of the enterprise. And this in turn requires one-time expenditures that are incomparably larger than with ordinary reconstruction involving partial alterations of buildings. Furthermore, there would be a need for investments in the creation and retooling of existing enterprises the related branches of the construction industry and construction materials The very idea of a steady decline in the passive share of fixed capital is not viable. It stands in contradiction to technical progress, which is causing fundamental changes in the functional load on buildings and structures.

According to the logic of things, the improvement of the technical structure of fixed capital should have involved not a contraposing but a blending of the active and passive components of fixed capital. The distinctions between them are in practice being eroded. A growing number of the structural components and types of engineering equipment of buildings perform some sort of active technological function, for example, ceiling braces that support cranes, air conditioning systems, etc. With the development of chemical and other industrial processes, the significance of structures such as settling basins, thickening tanks, cooling towers, etc., and various pipelines, conveyer belts, gas flues, and gas purifiers has increased, i.e., assets that have a direct technological function but are considered "structures" in Soviet statistics only because of their construction origins and thus fall in the category of passive fixed capital. Structures in the fuel and mining branches of industry play an exceptional role in production technology. Classifying such structures as oil wells and mine shafts in these branches as passive fixed capital is totally inappropriate.

In objectively evaluating the trend in the technical structure of capital, it should be noted that the increase in the passive share does not in the least mean a reduction in economic efficiency. It may be just the opposite. The effort to minimize the size of buildings leads in many cases to a decline in production efficiency. When, for example, a cement plant was constructed in the Urals with open-air klinker ovens (as was done in Uzbekistan), fuel expenditures increased sharply in the winter because the oven walls cooled down too much. Capital investments per ton of cement were lower than in comparable plants in the Urals where ovens were enclosed. But the growth in production expenditures due to fuel costs turned out to be so substantial that the overall effectiveness of capital investment in these plants could not withstand comparison with normative coefficients.

Thus it is fair to conclude that the increase in the scale of the rebuilding and modernization of industrial structures during the reconstruction of Soviet industry is a quite natural phenomenon. But this also results in the increase in the amount of construction-installation work, the cost and labor-intensiveness of which is much higher in existing enterprises than in the construction of new ones. Standard designs are not used for reconstruction, the level of mechanization is much lower, and prefabricated components are used to a lesser extent. Labor expenditures in the reconstruction of automobile plants, for example, are 60 percent higher than in the construction of new plants.[28] Expenditures of materials are higher by a similar amount.[29] For industrial construction in the machine-building and metalworking branch, the labor/output ratio for construction-installation work in the expansion and reconstruction of existing enterprises is 1.23-1.35 times higher than in the construction of new enterprises.[30]

---

[28]N. Budunova, *Effektivnost' kapital'nykh vlozhenii i rekonstruktsiia v promyshlennosti.* Moscow: Stroiizdat, 1978, p. 193.
[29]Ibid., p. 194.
[30]T. Bakaeva and V. Zadorozhnyi, "Uchet vliianiia strukturnykh sdvigov na vyrabotku v stroitel'stve," *Vestnik statistiki,* 1977, no. 10, p. 18.

Another not unimportant factor that contributes to the higher cost of reconstruction work and lengthens project completion times is the insufficient number of construction-installation enterprises undertaking such work because they have no material incentives to do it. Therefore, the reconstruction of buildings and structures is most often carried out by small-scale repair-construction divisions of the enterprises themselves, and they are undercapitalized and operate with low labor productivity.

THE TEMPO AND QUALITATIVE LEVEL OF EQUIPMENT RENOVATION

Before we evaluate the results of the Soviet policy of mainly investing in the modernization of existing enterprises, let us pose the most important question: is the withdrawal of old technologies and machines proceeding at a faster pace, and are they being replaced with equipment which is *really* new and which permits not only an increase in the volume of production but also perfection of its qualitative level? It is important to bear in mind here that writing off fixed capital at an accelerated pace should have been facilitated by the amortization reform of 1975, which noticeably curtailed the service life of fixed capital. Thus, has the replacement of machines and equipment been speeded up? The writing off of fixed capital stock on the whole actually dropped off somewhat (in relative terms) in the 1970s from 1.8 percent in 1970 to 1.4 percent in 1980. Over the course of the decade the yearly writing off of equipment stayed at a level of 2.4-2.5 percent. With the introduction of new rates of amortization, the only thing that increased was the gap between scheduled and actual writing off of equipment.

According to calculations by Soviet specialists, actual writing-off of industrial fixed capital should be twice the 1979-80 level of 1.4 percent.[31] In the late 1970s, achievement of the amortization goals would have required a tripling of actual write-offs of equipment. However, the machine-building industry—undercapitalized and oriented predominantly toward equipping new production capacities—was not capable of producing either the amount or the proper types of machinery to sustain such a program of equipment replacement (more on this below).

If we base our analysis on official statistics, we have to draw the conclusion that the expected acceleration of equipment withdrawal not only has not taken place but that this process has decelerated.

---

[31] *Narkhoz 1970*, p. 169; *Narkhoz 1980*, p. 147; V. Senchagov and V. Ostapenko, "The Significance of Amortization in Technical Renovation," *Voprosy ekonomiki.* Moscow, no. 1, 1981, pp. 34, 37.

However, official statistics give information only for the withdrawal of fixed capital because of "decay, wear and tear, and elemental disasters." They do not reflect the writing off of under-amortized equipment which is written off in the course the modernization and reconstruction of enterprises. If we include this aspect of replacement as well, the picture becomes much more dynamic.

Perhaps the most reliable starting point for determining the total volume of the writing-off of equipment is Kvasha's study of this question,[32] which used data of the general inventories of fixed capital in industry in 1962 and 1972. Kvasha who was a very qualified specialist, compiled a sample of various types of industrial equipment that was not only representative but unique in the history of Soviet industrial statistics. It included more than 35 percent of all equipment in Soviet industry. As a result of his calculations the retirement coefficient for 1962-71 was determined to be 4.4 percent per year in terms of number of machines and 4.3 percent in terms of value. Taking into account some additional factors, Kvasha revised this average coefficient to 4.2 percent.

Kvasha's results refute the general impression about the insufficient level of retirement of equipment in Soviet industry. Other researchers, basing their calculations on manipulations of data in Soviet statistical handbooks,[33] obtain a significantly lower coefficient of retirement—2.1 or 2.5 percent The reason for the discrepancy is that Kvasha, working with concrete plant-level statistics, took into account not only the retirement of equipment for reasons of physical wear and tear (for which there are data in statistical handbooks) but also the equipment written off that had not yet exceeded its service life but was written off in the process of renovation.

The fact that a large amount of unamortized equipment is written off in the process of renovation is confirmed by the results of a study made by the experimental scientific-research institute of metal-cutting machinery, which encompassed various machine-building plants with a total of 228,000 metal-cutting machines.[34] The study showed that about 40 percent of the machines retired were less than 15 years old, i.e., less than the standard service life, while 23 percent were less than 10 years old. In the group "less than 10 years," about 60 percent of the machines were written off not because of physical wear and tear but because they were obsolete, unsuitable for production, or of an

---

[32]Kvasha, "Teknicheskii," 1976, p. 131.
[33]Iu. Kurenkov and D. Palterovich, *Technicheskii progress i optimal'noe obnovlenie proizvodstvennogo apparata*. Moscow: Mysl', 1975, pp. 49-52; Smyshliaeva, *Ekonomicheskii*, 1976, p. 146.
[34]Kurenkov and Palterovich, *Tekhnicheskii*, 1975, pp. 58-60.

inappropriate design, i.e., for subjective reasons. Note the following paradoxic fact: 24.6 percent of the machines in the "less than 10 years" group were written off because of obsolescence, while the corresponding proportion for all groups over 10 years was only 7.1 percent. When equipment that does not exceed the standard service life is written off during reconstruction, "obsolescence" is a convenient justification for writing it off.

It is unlikely that obsolescence is the real reason for writing off equipment that is not very old given the strict limitations on the amount of new equipment and the existing correllation between the productivity and cost of new models—with each one percent increase in the productivity of new machines the price increases 2-4 percent.[35] The extent to which fundamentally new electric, electrochemical, and laser methods of metalworking are used is expanding very slowly. Only 0.2-0.3 percent of all machines had numerically programmed controls at the beginning of the 1970s. Therefore the share of equipment retired because of obsolescence should be insignificant.

Enterprises are trying under the flag of reconstruction to use any means to write off as much equipment as possible (or sell or transfer it to other enterprises) and to receive as replacements new equipment financed by investment flows if possible. Savings on repair more than offset the increased depreciation charges and payments for fixed capital associated with introducing new and more expensive equipment.

These conclusions are supported by studies done by V. Fal'tsman at the Central Mathematical-Economics Institute that involved calculations of the actual indicators of trends in the growth and renewal of the country's stock of equipment.[36] The replacement coefficient (the share of the total value of equipment that is replaced) was 4.9 percent for Soviet industry in 1971-75. We can assume that during the time period covered by Fal'tsman's calculations (compared with Kvasha's period) the rate at which equipment was retired increased.

A study of the structure of investment flows for equipment in the 1970s showed that the share of expenditures for replacement for various types of equipment was (in percent): hoisting-transporting equipment—52.0, metallurgical equipment—52.9, drilling equipment—66.3, chemical equipment—35.0, and instruments—39.2.[37] Thus roughly half of equipment goes to replace withdrawals.

---

[35]Ibid., p. 61.
[36]Fal'tsman, "Intensifikatsiia," 1978, p. 26.
[37]Ibid., p. 29.

In sum, the growth of reconstruction leads to more intensified replacement of equipment. Let us try now to examine not the quantitative but the qualitative aspect of updating the equipment stock: to what extent is new technology used in replacing equipment and does the newly installed equipment make possible lower capital and current production expenditures?

The possibilities for replacing discarded equipment with new types of machinery decreased in absolute terms during the second half of the 1970s. According to official Soviet statistics the number of models of new types of equipment developed on the average each year declined by 8 percent during 1976-80 as compared with 1971-75.[38] At the same time the total output of machine building increased. Apparently, the flow of new technology into industry is declining at the same time as machinery is being replaced more rapidly. It should also be considered that newly constructed enterprises have priority in receiving new, more productive equipment,[39] and the replacement of equipment retired during reconstruction largely involves traditional and improved equipment. The new equipment in many instances has no technical or economic advantages over that which it replaces.[40]

The problem is that the number of types of various machines produced is very limited; the parameters of equipment are overly standardized and not oriented to the individual needs of any given enterprise. And the development of unique, non-mass-produced types of equipment is an extremely complex matter under conditions of the Soviet planned distribution system for allocating orders to enterprises. The creation of non-mass-produced equipment by enterprises themselves has reached substantial proportions as the 1972 census of equipment showed.[41] But the technical characteristics of such equipment are, as a rule much lower than for similar types produced at specialized machine-building enterprises. It is primarily enterprises or construction projects that are especially important to the national economy—above all, of course, the defense industry—that have the possibility of submitting orders for large-scale non-mass-produced equipment. Therefore, many enterprises are faced with a choice: either introduce mass-produced equipment into the framework of the existing enterprise, rebuilding structures to accommodate it, and reworking the system of communications and power supply, or partially modernize existing

---

[38] *Narkhoz 1980*, p. 100.
[39] Kvasha, *Tekhnicheskii*, 1976, p. 180.
[40] Ibid.
[41] A. Sidorov and V. Gumeniuk, "Sovershenstvovanie organizatsionnykh form proizvodstva nestandartnogo oborudovaniia," in *Effektivnost' osnovnykh fondov, kapital'nykh vlozhenii i novoi tekhniki*. Kiev: Institut ekonomiki AN UkSSR, 1975, p. 199.

equipment, retaining the old technological base, but trying to increase its productivity. In cases where reconstruction requires updating large stationary machines or assemblies, many enterprises prefer just this approach. The extent of modernization of equipment is systematically growing. The average number of units of equipment modernized in industry were (in thousands) 135 in 1966-70, 146 in 1971-75, and 162 in 1976-80.[42]

The process of updating equipment in reconstructing an enterprise largely involves retirement and replacment with new models for general types of production equipment and the partial modernization of specialized basic technological equipment that is specific to a particular type of production. Such modernization leads primarily to an increase in technical measures of productivity (e.g., output per hour), but does not have a positive effect on improving other economic indicators.

As noted above, the branch of industry with the highest share of capital investment in reconstruction of existing enterprises is ferrous metallurgy (over 80 percent). What sort of possibilities are there for reconstruction involving the introduction of fundamentally new equipment and technology in this key branch of heavy industry, whose lagging development hinders the entire Soviet economy?[43] Characterizing technological innovations in production, the well-known Soviet specialists in metallurgy A. Vertman and E. Kalinnikov note that of the two most significant innovations in the branch developed by Soviet scholars in 1950 (the continuous steel casting process) and in 1960 (combining continuous pouring with rolling), as of 1974 not one was introduced into production, and even development under industrial conditions had not begun.[44] The authors believe that the reason for the low level of development and introduction of new technology in the branch is the "underestimation of the role and insufficient development of fundamental research." A comparison they make is evidence of this only 0.5 percent of those employed in ferrous metallurgy in the USSR work in the sphere of scientific research, while in the Krupp firm of West Germany the corresponding share is 3 percent.

Certainly some examples of the development and introduction of new types of equipment and new technologies can be cited in such high-priority branches of industry as oil and petrochemicals, gas, and instrument building. But they do not set the general tone. The more typical situation is that in ferrous metallurgy.

---

[42] *Narhoz 1980*, p. 102.
[43] *Partiinaia zhizn'*, 1978, no. 23, p. 6.
[44] A. Vertman and E. Kalinnikov, "Chernaia metallurgia: alternativy razvitiia," *Ekonomika i organizatsiia promyshlennogo proizvodstva*, 1976, no. 3, pp. 41-45.

Only in those cases when an increase in capacity at existing enterprises is attained through a radical change in technology and production equipment is there a tangible reduction in capital and current expenditures per unit increase in output. Then the cost of rebuilding buildings and structures, expanding production floor-space, communications, and the transportation network, and constructing new shops is recouped. Soviet economists also make this point.[45]

Capital expenditures to increase the unit productivity of equipment in Soviet industry are growing systematically. And they are growing not only in cases where higher productivity is accompanied by improvements in the technical-economic and ergonomic parameters of equipment, but also in cases where no such improvement takes place. At the same time in many instances the weight of equipment is growing at a faster rate due to the enlargement of models.[46] Thus, the more frequent case is the extensive development of equipment, which makes it possible to expand production capacities although reducing economic gains in the form of lower capital expenditures. Let us explain this with an example. According to data of the state institute for the design of heavy machine-building enterprises, with an increase in the capacity of power blocks of thermal power stations from 25,000 to 50,000 kilowatts, the cost of equipment per kilowatt of capacity was reduced by 29 percent, while with an increase in capacity from 200,000 to 300,000 kilowatts, the reduction in relative expenditures on equipment was only 3-5 percent and relative expenditures on electric power equipment remained unchanged.[47]

Such instances of diminishing savings of expenditures with increasing capacity are characteristic of the development of equipment in many industrial branches: chemical, food, construction materials, and others.[48]

The effect of the introduction of new equipment and technology on reducing current production expenditures in Soviet industry as a whole can be judged from changes in expenditures per ruble of commodity output in industry, which were (in constant prices, as a percentage of the previous year): -1.0 in 1970, -0.7 in 1975, and -0.1 in 1980.[49] In examining the trend in the change in expenditures for industry as a

---

[45]T. Khachaturov, *Effektivnost' kapital'nykh vlozhenii.* Moscow: Ekonomika, 1979, p. 61.
[46]Krasovskii, "Ekonomicheskie," 1980, pp. 108-110; V. Cheplanov, "Faktory effektivnosti proizvodstva chernykh metallov," *Ekonomika i organizatsiia promyshlennogo proizvodstva,* 1977, no. 3, pp. 135-137; M. Vorobievskii et al., *Povyshenie effektivnosti kapital'nykh vlozhenii i osnovnykh fondov v promyshlennosti stroimaterialov.* Moscow: Stroiizdat, 1975, p. 273.
[47]Palterovich, *Park,* 1970, p. 71.
[48]Ibid., p. 71.
[49]*Narkhoz 1970,* p. 173; *Narkhoz 1980,* p. 152.

whole, it should be kept in mind that changes in the branch structure of industry had no effect.

The gains realized in the form of a reduction in the enterprise cost of production as a result of the updating of the production apparatus are decreasing.

And so, it seems justified to conclude that the writing-off of equipment is going on much more intensely than one might suppose from official statistics. Apparently there is a tendency evolving whereby underamortized equipment which has not attained its normal service life is written off. It seems to us that the explanations for this phenomenon are the following:

- the withdrawal of underamortized equipment from exploitation is conditioned both by its low technological level and design quality of metal;

- the conditions of global renovation create a favorable climate the premature withdrawal of equipment and its replacement through procurements based on capital investments.

As for the amortization reform, it has not had any substantive effect on the acceleration of technology renovation. For all intents and purposes, the most important consideration in writing off equipment is not its normal service life, but whether one can get new replacements for it under the flag of reconstruction.

Even without sufficient data, nevertheless we see the grounds for the following hypothesis: to a significant extent, relatively new equipment is being written off under the flag of renovation, while on the whole writing off through wear and tear and decay proceeds sluggishly. This in no way meets the expectations of the authors of the amortization reform of 1975. Can we expect the further liberalization of amortization policy and practical support for it in the near future?

Basing our analysis on any number of Soviet publications, in view of the dynamics of technological progress, we can suppose that the rates of amortization in Soviet industry should be reviewed every ten years.[50] The interval between the last two amortization reforms was twelve years (1963 and 1975). Judging by the number of convincing signs,[51] however, the new amortization form cannot be implemented earlier than the second half of the 1980s. Thus, retaining the existing

---

[50]D. Palterovich, "Obnovlenie oborudovaniya i tekhnicheskoe perevooruzhenie proizvodstva," *Planovoe khozyaistvo*, no. 9, 1980, p. 104.
[51]M. Zavalishin, A. Malygin, "O pereotsenke osnovnykh fondov i utochenenii norm amortizatsii," *Planovoe khozyaistvo*, no. 6, 1981.

amortization norms in the first half of the '80s will not stimulate more intensive renovation of fixed capital stock through replacement.

But even the existing guidelines for attaining the rates of writing off equipment scheduled for the 1980s, it is necessary to increase the write-off of fixed capital stock more than three times the actual level of the late '70s. Neither the present level of machine-building production nor its specialization, which is predominantly oriented toward equipping new productive capacities, even approximates such a requirement.

Let us now consider another important question: is the replacement of the withdrawn equipment being implemented on a qualitatively new level? Is the share of really new equipment within replacement technology increasing? The dynamics of renovating the output of the Soviet machine-building industry show that the very potential for expanding the scope of equipment replacement on a new scientific and technical framework is being reduced. In the output of some machine-building industries, the share of products which take five years or less to produce was 55 percent in 1967, while in 1978 it was 42 percent.[52] The share of products which take more than ten years to manufacture rose in the same period from 16 percent to 27 percent. Furthermore, do products newly approved for production possess any real novelty, if only for the USSR? That is, are the things being accepted in the USSR for the first time? In 1973, 48 percent of the output of the machine-building industry conformed to this stipulation, while in 1978 only 39.5 percent did.[53]

No less telling an indicator of the development of the technological level of the Soviet machine-building industry is how many new kinds of equipment are created annually. In the latter part of the 1970s on the whole, there was a drop in the number of prototypes for various kinds of new machinery being created This included a 27 percent reduction in energy-related equipment, a 12 percent reduction in machine tools, a 20 percent reduction in equipment for metallurgy, and a reduction of 15 percent in chemical equipment.[54] Particularly sensitive for industrial technological progress is the drop in the number of new models in the precision machine-building industries: instrument making, automation devices, and computer science.

Replacement is taking place chiefly on the basis of an improved, partially perfected technology, but with the old technological foundation and the old technological plans and methods of production.

---

[52]D. Palterovich, "Obnovlenie ...," p. 104.
[53]Ibid.
[54]*Narkhoz 1980*, pp. 100-101.

As regards receiving new (and not renovated) technology, industry has been on starvation rations, and the situation in recent years has taken an abrupt turn for the worse. Consequently, the role of major overhauls has grown not only in maintenance, but also in the partial modernization of equipment, despite the fact that the share of major overhauls in the 1975 amortization rates was lowered.

For example, capital investments in ferrous mettalurgy totalled 2.2 billion rubles in 1970, while expenditures on major overhauls totalled 694 million or 32 percent. In 1978, these numbers were 3.1 and 1.28 billion respectively, or 42 percent.[55]

Thus, instead of replacing old equipment with new, it is repaired many times, restored while retaining the old technological foundation.

SPEEDING UP CAPITAL TURNOVER BY REDUCING THE AMOUNT OF TIME NEEDED FOR THE CREATION AND BREAKING IN OF PRODUCTIVE CAPACITIES

It had seemed obvious that a positive result of the policy by which the share of investments in already existing enterprises was increased would be a natural shortening of the time between when investments are realized and when there is an increment in output. Inordinately prolonged periods needed for construction and the breaking in of newly introduced productive capacities are an immanent characteristic of the Soviet investment process; indeed, discussion of the need for shortening these time periods (and the grave consequences in store for the Soviet economy if this is not done) has been a de rigueur topic of innumerable congresses and conferences, starting with the very first years of Soviet power. Did the Soviet Union manage to speed up the construction in the 1970s by transferring investments from new construction to renovation? Did it succeed in bringing the incrementing output closer to the moment of investment?

What has occurred is not a shortening, but on the contrary, a lengthening of construction periods. Testifying to this is the fact that the volume of unfinished industrial construction more than doubled over the decade, while as regards annual capital investments it increased from 73 percent to 87 percent.[56]

As for the time necessary for breaking in newly introduced productive capacities, reality did not match expectations here, either the relation of increment in output to increment capacity took a sharp turn for the worse in the second half of the '70s as compared to the first

---

[55] V. Krasovsky, "Tekhnicheskoe perevooruzhenie proizvodstva i effektivnost' remonta," *Voprosy ekonomiki*, no. 7, 1981, p. 32.
[56] *Narkhoz 1980*, p. 345.

half.

In only two of the items listed in the table below did the increment in output grow in relation to the increment in productive capacity in the second half of the '70s; in all the others, it dropped. In the coal industry between 1976 and 1980, the increment in productive capacities for coal output was 90.4 million tons while the actual increment in output was only 15 million tons. In the chemical industry, an increment in capacities for the production of sulphuric acid of 9.7 million tons corresponded to an increment in production of 4.4 million tons; in the production of soda ash, this relationship was 505 and 88 thousand tons, respectively; and in the production of mineral fertilizers, it was 39.3 and 13.8 million tons (in conventional units).[57]

Table 1

THE RELATION OF INCREMENT IN OUTPUT TO INCREMENT IN PRODUCTION CAPACITIES[58]

	1971-1975	1976-1980
Pig Iron	1.32	0.71
Steel	2.29	0.49
Rolled ferrous metal	1.47	0.58
Steel pipes	1.51	1.16
Sulphuric acid	0.75	0.45
Mineral fertilizers (in conventional units)	0.91	0.35
Plastics and synthetic resins	1.19	0.53
Fibers and chemical fibers	0.95	0.95
Automobile tires	1.31	0.65
Turbines	0.48	0.46
Automobiles (including buses)	1.07	0.96
Excavators	1.22	0.22
Cellulose	0.81	0.33
Paper	2.02	0.26
Cement	1.29	0.27
Knitted underwear and outer garments	1.18	3.20
Leather footwear	0.28	2.13

[57]Ibid.
[58]G. Pavlov, L. Pchelkina, "Balansy proizvodstvennykh moshchnostei—osnova razrabotki plana proizvodstva," *Planovoe khoziyaistvo*, no. 9, 1981, p. 46.

In the machine-tool industry, productive capacities were put into operation for an increment of 12.5 thousand machine tools, but in actual fact the industry tolerated a drop in production of 15,000 units. In eight of the seventeen items, the increment on output came to less than 50 percent of the increment in capacities.[59] The reasons for the increase in unused productive potential, combined with the huge and growing output deficit, are numerous and varied. Among them we may note the languishing of the raw materials industries and inadequacies of transport conditioned by the growing distance between where the raw materials are produced and where they are used; irregularities in fuel deliveries; and finally, the growing lack of control over the economy as a whole.

But all of these factors are of a general economic and even political nature. The concrete reasons are these: the fact that technologically interconnected productive components are not put into operation simultaneously; the fact that the exploitation of accessory objects intended for use throughout a plant lags behind the basic technological objects; and the fact that enterprises are forced to move ahead with production even when bottlenecks at certain stages of the production line are holding output levels down. For example, the years after blooming mill N° 1150 of the Krivoi Rog (Ukraine) metallurgy works was put into operation, it for the most part attained only 70 percent of its projected capacities because of the inadequate capacity of the furnace installations.[60] The blooming mill was working with only eight pit-furnace complexes, and it would be possible to cite numerous examples.

REASONS FOR THE FAILURE OF THE RECONSTRUCTION POLICY

Thus not one of the goals of the reconstruction policy which was underway in the 1970s was met. They did not succeed in attaining either the increase and speeding up of the increment in output, or the saving of resources. They did not succeed in making the investment process more healthy. The policy slowed down technological progress in industry. In the second half of the '70s the capital intensity of industrial production almost doubled as compared to the first half, while the annual rate of increase in labor productivity in industry fell by almost 200 percent.

[59]Ibid.
[60]V. Krasovsky, "Investitsionnyi kompleks; planirovanie i reservy," *Voprosy ekonomiki*, no. 1, 1979.

The reason for the failure is that the economy's investment sphere was totally unprepared for such a large-scale program. The corresponding scientific, design, planning, and machine-building bases were not re-oriented or prepared. The construction industry was not reorganized, nor was it equipped to engage in renovations. Finally, no one established the kind of material stimulation which would encourage people toward more labor-intensive work in already functioning enterprises, the kind of stimulation which would compensate for running the risk of not fulfilling the production plan, with all the material consequences resulting therefrom.

The idea of reconstruction, per se, considered as the technical renovation of existing enterprises on a more modern basis, which makes it possible to increase production and reduce costs with relatively low capital expenditures, is quite positive and commonly accepted. It is particularly appropriate in a period of declining investment growth. But this idea in its pure form must be distinguished from its implementation in the concrete conditions of the current state of the Soviet economy.

In establishing the advantages of reconstruction and the need for its further development, the leaders of the Soviet economy cite foreign, and above all American, experience. Academician Khachaturov, for example, in a monograph published in 1979,[61] carefully noted the unfavorable aspects of reconstruction but argued nonetheless in the following way for the need to expand it: "The share of reconstruction in capital investment in our economy is growing, but it is still lower than in developed capitalist countries, above all in the USA."

Data on the amount of investment in reconstruction in US industry used in Soviet sources are taken primarily from the annual McGraw-Hill survey of business plans for new plant and equipment. However, we do not think that the data given in these publications do not correspond to the data of the Soviet Central Statistical Administration on the amount of capital investment in "reconstruction, expansion, and retooling of existing enterprises" either according to definition or to the methodology of distributing capital expenditures. But even if these data are used, expenditures on modernization and replacement did not exceed 56 percent of the total amount of investment in the manufacturing industry in the USA in 1976-78.[62] What can there be in common between the reconstruction of industrial enterprises in the USSR and the USA? They have nothing in common with

[61] Khachaturov, *Effektivnosat'*, *1979*, p. 61.
[62] *28th Annual McGraw-Hill Survey, Business Plans for New Plants and Equipment, 1975-1978*. New York: McGraw-Hill, 1975.

respect to either the material, technical, and construction base, or the method of carrying out reconstruction, or the availability of labor resources. In the USSR the primary aim of reconstruction is to increase the volume of output, while in the USA it is to improve or change qualitative characteristics or to reduce production costs. In the USSR the share of equipment in fixed capital in 1975 was 35 percent; in the USA it was 87 percent.[63] Thus, the character of production processes, the technical composition of capital, and the availability and level of technical progress in producers' goods are so different in the two countries that comparison makes little sense.

Together with difficulties of an economic nature, organizational and methodological problems that arise in the planning of reconstruction work should also be mentioned. These problems are connected with the impossibility of standardizing the varied types of reconstruction of enterprises that arise due to the unique conditions of each individual plant or factory. Attempts to develop a system of norms for expenditures of capital investments and other resources per unit increase in capacity from reconstruction have led nowhere. There is a lack of coordination in the basic methodological guidelines. To date there is still no fixed definition of the criteria of economic effectiveness for reconstruction. And without a methodic and normative base—the fundamental instrument of planning—attempts to regulate and control capital investments in existing production facilities and to evaluate the economic benefits of such investments prove unsuccessful. In putting a stake in reconstruction in forming their investment policy, Soviet planners did not take into account the fact that it would encompass such a large share of not only the active but passive components of fixed capital. The maximum permissible coefficient of renewal of assets under reconstruction according to guidelines of the Institute of Economics of the Academy of Sciences is 0.5.[64] However, in practice this coefficient frequently reaches 0.8.[65]

Generalizing the experience of reconstruction of industry in the USSR, a leading Soviet specialist in the economics of capital investment, academician Khachaturov, wrote in the work cited above: "Reconstruction is effective when the replacement of equipment with more modern equipment does not require substantial and expensive construction-installation work."

---

[63]Ibid.
[64]Institut ekonomiki AN SSSR, Ural'skii nauchnyi tsentr AN SSSR, *Metodicheskie polozheniia po opredeleniiu ekonomicheskoi effektivnosti kapital'nykh vlozhenii na rekonstruktsiiu i rasshirenie deistvuiushchikh promyshlennykh predpriiatii*. Sverdlovsk, 1975, p. 5.
[65]Budunova, *Effektivnost'*, 1978, p. 199.

Though one may agree with this thesis, in light of the facts discussed above it is impossible to consider the reconstruction that has been carried out in the Soviet Union effective.

However, it is impossible to admit that the most important party directives on economic policy proved to be poorly thought out and badly prepared. The press, the party decrees, and the planning sector kept demanding the largest possible increases in investments in the renovation and modernization of industry. Without material support, however, these appeals are left hanging in mid-air:

- design organizations for the most part concentrate on designing new enterprises—standard serial projects which are easier and more profitable for them;

- standardized equipment, not machines made to fit the specific conditions and dimensions of an enterprise under renovation;

- builders exert the most strenuous efforts to avoid contracts for reconstruction work, the labor intensity of which is 20 percent higher than in new construction, and the earnings four times less.[66]

The simple and (it would seem) judicious idea of renovation could not withstand the ordeal of practice. As it was being realized, it was supplanted by a more viable palliative, "expansion," which in essence was nothing more than the addition of new shops, or the building of genuinely new enterprises on the grounds of those already in operation, or on adjacent territories.

The heads of the ministries and enterprises are well aware of all these phenomena In order to obtain capital investments from the government, they resort to camouflage under the flag of renovation, they carry out new construction, which is spatially attached to the old enterprise.

Expansion is preferable to renovation for clients and contractors alike. In doing this, they formally observe the political line of the party leadership and Gosplan, but at the same time, the client adds on new productive capacities while disturbing the normal production rhythm of the enterprise as little as possible. It is incomparably easier for the contractor to work on open building sites. Besides this, expansion gives the contractor much larger volumes of work.

[66]V. Danilov, "Uskorenie," *Pravda*, 17 December, 1980.

Of course, expansion demands more significant expenditures of labor for an increment in output than does renovation. But even under the present conditions of a growing labor deficit, this problem assumes secondary importance compared to investments. Capital remains the main concern of Soviet "executives." Vadim Kirichenko, the director of the Gosplan Scientific Institute, made the following observation in this regard in 1981:

> One can sense inertia of economic thinking, in accordance with which the most important thing is to create capital stock, to erect new objects; meanwhile, the feeling is that labor can be found anywhere.[67]

Thus Soviet industrial executives circumvent Gosplan regulations like rivers flowing around boulders which lie in their path.

Official statistics conceal the fact that the predominant form in which capital investments are utilized is not "renovation and technological re-equipping," but rather "expansion."

Expansion, however, is being carried out under circumstances in which the technological resources of the Soviet machine-building industry are shrinking; in which the opportunities for importing advanced technology are extremely limited; and in which raw material, energy, and ecological factors in the European part of the USSR (where most of Soviet industry is concentrated) are becoming increasingly restricted. Expansion thus represents an extensive, resource-wasting way to increase productive potential.

THE REDUCTION IN THE SHARE OF NET INVESTMENT AND SOME THEORETICAL EXERCISES ON THE PART OF SOVIET ECONOMISTS

A natural consequence of the renovation taking place in Soviet industry, is the restructuring of industrial capital investment: the growth of the share of expenditures on replacement and, correspondingly, the reduction in the share of net capital investment—for expansion.

Misgivings about this correlation between net new investment and replacement investment during a period of declining rates of economic growth began to appear among Soviet economists especially in the early 1970s. Given the decline in rates of growth of gross social product and national income (and now declines in absolute increments as well) and the stabilization of the share allocated for capital accumulation, they have studied the possibilities of using depreciation payments for

---

[67]V. Kirichenko, "Odinnadtsataya pyatiletka: strukturnyesdvigi v ekonomike," *Izvestiya Akademiya nauk SSSR, seriya ekonomicheskaya,* 1981, no. 2, p. 8.

expanding the production base. All the more so since such a use of depreciation payments corresponds fully with the Marxist scheme of reproduction. And there is growing interest not so much in the distribution of capital investment between "net" and "compensatory" as in determining what portion of total depreciation allowances can be used not for replacement but for the expansion of fixed capital.

Just this effort to gain an understanding of economic process when greater significance is given to depreciation allowances as a source of expanding the economy explains the growing interest in work done by E. Domar in the early 1950s[68] and the attempts to use his work as a starting point in developing a new concept. The essence of this concept is that it is by no means necessary that a reduction in investment out of national income must lead to a decline in rates of economic growth. The decline in the growth of capital investment resulting from reduced rates of growth of (and absolute increments to) national income can be offset from the excess of depreciation allowances over requirements for replacing fixed capital each year.[69]

This idea is supported using a model developed by Domar. An important prerequisite of the model, which makes it possible to apply it to the Soviet economy, is the assumption of straight-line depreciation with no scrap value. Soviet economists have introduced into Domar's model the condition that, unlike traditional models of economic growth where depreciation allowances (D) are equal to real replacement (R), depreciation allowances serve as an element of capital accumulation. In the interpretation of Soviet economists, Domar's model establishes the mathematical relation between the growth of the "final product" (P) (the sum of national income and depreciation) and the share of net investment (G − D, where G is gross investment) in national income. The growth of the final product P is proportional to the accumulation of fixed capital financed from both national income and depreciation. Therefore, the capital coefficient in this model is defined as $v = (G - R)/ \triangle P$, while in traditional growth models this coefficient is equal to $(G - D)/ \triangle (P - D)$, since the effect of increasing output is related only to net investment out of national income.

---

[68] Evsey D. Domar, *Essays in the Theory of Economic Growth*. New York: Oxford University Press, 1957.
[69] A. Notkin, "Nakoplenie i ego rol' v sotsialisticheskom vosproizvodstve," in *Sotsialisticheskoe nakoplenie*. Moscow: Nauka, 1973, pp. 35-36; N. Filonova, "Metodicheskie voprosy opredeleniia kapital'nykh vlozhenii na vozmeshchenie osnovnykh fondov," *Voprosy ekonomiki*, 1968, no. 9; A. Tsygichko, "Zamena sredstv truda v promyshlennosti SSSR i SShA," *Voprosy ekonomiki*, 1972, no. 10; and others.

Soviet economists focus their attention on excess depreciation allowances used for growth (D − R). They arrive at the optimistic conclusion that the value of (D − R) is growing and that the growth of fixed capital will increase as a result, compensating for a reduction in the possibilities of financing capital investment out of national income.

Is this feasible? The equations in Domar's model are essentially functions of the product of the service life of assets (r) and the rate of growth of capital investment (m). Given constant prices of fixed capital, the structure of gross capital investment depends only on two independent variables, r and m. However, as shown above, the price of fixed assets in the USSR is increasing. Domar explained that under conditions of increasing prices of fixed assets the disparity between D and R is reduced, i.e., a larger part of depreciation allowances is used for purposes of replacement than is the case when prices are constant. Changes in r and m are acting in the same direction in the USSR: the service life of producers' goods is being reduced in connection with the 1975 reform of depreciation rates, and the rates of investment, like their absolute increments, are also declining. This massive demand for unamortized fixed assets aggravates the reduction of the gap between D and R. Thus, calculations based on an increase in (D − R) are unfounded, and the possibility of increasing investment from depreciation allowances is not growing but, quite the opposite, declining.

According to calculations made using the real level of replacement estimated below and data on depreciation allowances in current prices, the ratio of actual expenditures on replacement to total depreciation charges (in percent) has been increasing as follows: 51 in 1970, 59 in 1975, and 60 in 1980.[70] If it is also taken into account that the prices of the fixed assets used as replacements are substantially higher than the book value or the replacement value (as a result of the 1972 reevaluation) of the replaced assets, then the gap between D and R is even smaller. (D − R), as a source of net investment, decreases in direct proportion to the acceleration of price increases on the output of investment branches and the reduction of the rate of investment growth.

Without pretending to achieve great accuracy, we will try to break down total capital investment into net and compensatory investment. In order to determine R, we will use the value of the coefficient of replacement of equipment obtained by Fal'tsman[71] for industry as a whole during 1971-1975—4.9. This coefficient, as mentioned above, seems to be the most reliable since it was calculated on the basis of firm-level data on equipment balances. The value 4.9 was determined

[70] *Narkhoz 1980*, p. 521.
[71] Fal'tsman, "Intensifikatsiia," 1978, p. 26.

as the average for 1971-75. But in 1975 a reform of depreciation was instituted, as a result of which depreciation allowances for renovation for industry as a whole increased 40 percent, and the average service life of productive fixed assets in industry was reduced from 25.6 to 21.3 years or by 16.8 percent.[72] The rate of retirement of fixed assets did not increase to an extent corresponding to this reduction in service life, but it did increase.

There is a significant gap between the theory and practice of depreciation in the USSR—between its accounting and actual aspects. A financial base for speeding up the replacement of equipment is being created. However, it does not correspond to physical resources: balances of the production and distribution of the output of investment branches do not allow a sufficient quantity for replacement. Just this is the reason for the paradoxical situation that service life was reduced while the share of fixed assets due to wear and tear (according to official statistics) increased only slightly: 1.4 percent in 1974, 1.6 in 1975, and 1.4 in 1980.[73] This is true of both active and passive components of fixed capital. But, as noted above, official statistics do not reflect the real retirement of fixed capital. After the introduction of new depreciation rates, it must have speeded up since the consequences of writing off unamortized assets during reconstruction became less painful for enterprises. It should be correct to assume that, given all of the circumstances discussed, the coefficient of replacement of equipment increased from 4.9 in 1975 to at least 6.0 by 1980. At the same time, given the difference of 0.7 percentage points between Kvasha's data,[74] which relate to 1962-72, and Fal'tsman's for 1971-75, we will use a coefficient of 4.2 for 1970. With these coefficients of equipment replacement of 4.2, 4.9, and 6.0 for 1970, 1975, and 1980, respectively, we can determine the share of capital investment in equipment that is used for replacement.

It is more difficult to determine the replacement share of capital investment in passive assets. However, it seems possible to do this on the basis of the relation between active and passive components in the overall amount of assets retired. As already mentioned, data of this type that are published in the statistical yearbooks do not reflect the true state of affairs. According to estimates of the deputy director of the Institute of the Economics of Construction attached to the Moscow Engineering-Construction Institute, R. Merkin, the share of buildings and structures in the total value of fixed capital retired in machine

---

[72] Zavalishin and Masal'skii, "Novye," 1978, p. 66.
[73] *Narkhoz 1974*, p. 205; *Narkhoz 1975*, p. 225; *Narkhoz 1976*, p. 190.
[74] Kvasha, "Tekhnicheskii," 1976, p. 131.

building in 1970 was 27.2 percent.[75] As an indication of the lack of correspondence of the official data on the retirement of passive assets to the real situation, the share of buildings and structures retired due to wear and tear in machine building in 1973 (the first year for which such data were published) was reported to be only 2 percent.[76]

In branches of the construction materials industry the actual share of passive assets withdrawn during 1969-72 was 30-33 percent.[77]

As stated above, the share of passive assets in the total value of capital retired increases porportionately with the expansion of the scale of reconstruction. On this basis, we will assume the following hypothetical relations of passive to active assets in fixed capital retired: 30:70 for 1970, 40:60 for 1975, and 45:55 for 1980.

Calculations of the expenditures on replacement of fixed capital retired are given in table 2.

The continuing decline in net investment $(G - R)/G$, both in absolute and relative terms, and the growth of compensatory expenditures, R, leads to a slowing of the expansion of the productive potential of industry and, thus, to a reduction in the size of increments to the final product, ΔP.

In broad terms, the restructuring of the investment mechanism in the direction of reinvestment which took place during the 1970s was a natural process that was conditioned by the nature of previous stages of economic development in the USSR. During the period of industrialization (the 1930s), investment policy was based on new construction. Between 1924/25 and 1932/35, the share of new construction in the total amount of industrial capital investment increased from 14.2 to 46.3 percent,[78] which became possible because of an increase in the share of capital accumulation in national income during that period from 15.9 to 26.9 percent.[79] Even in those years an imbalance arose between financial resources and the physical possibilities for capital construction. Given such high rates of growth under conditions of extremely strained investment resources, the low technical level of construction and installation work, and the strict limitations on investment in passive assets, the quality of the capital created—especially industrial facilities—was very low.

---

[75]R. Merkin, "Sovershenstvovanie planirovaniia struktury kapital'nykh vlozhenii," *Izvestiia AN SSR, seriia ekonomicheskaia*, 1974, no. 4, p. 95.
[76]*Narkhoz 1973*, pp. 241, 238, 57.
[77]Author's personal experience.
[78]Barun, *Osnovnoi*, 1930, p. 265; Notkin, *Ocherki*, 1948, p. 202.
[79]Notkin, *Ocherki*, 1948, p. 171.

Table 2

CALCULATION OF ACTUAL CAPITAL EXPENDITURES ON REPLACEMENT[80]

	1970	1975	1980
1. Industrial fixed capital in constant prices (billions of rubles)	255	385	551
2. Share of equipment in industrial fixed capital (percent)	34.8	36	39.1
3. Value of equipment (billions of rubles)	88.7	138.6	215.4
4. Share of replaced equipment (percent)	4.2	4.9	6.0
5. Value of replaced equipment (billions of rubles)	3.7	6.8	12.9
6. Share of buildings and structures in fixed capital replaced (percent)	30	40	45
7. Value of replaced buildings and structures (billions of rubles)	1.6	4.5	10.5
8. Total value of fixed capital replaced (billions of rubles)	5.3	11.3	23.4
9. Capital investment in industry in constant prices (billions of rubles)	29.0	40.1	47.3
10. Share of capital investment for replacement (percent)	18.3	28.2	49.5
11. Rate of growth of gross industrial capital investment (1970=100)	100	138	162
12. Rate of growth of capital investment for replacement (1970=100)	100	154	270

The war had a very substantial effect on the condition of industrial fixed capital. Industrial enterprises evacuated to eastern regions of the country were located either in the buildings of old plants, with additions of buildings, structures, and communications facilities where extremely necessary, or in new sites involving new construction. In either case the construction and installation of the equipment shipped in was carried out during very difficult war-time conditions, in the shortest possible period of time, with many temporary structures, and without sufficient design and planning work. In subsequent years, allocations

[80] *Narkhoz 1978*, pp. 41, 130, 343; *Narkhoz 1965*, p. 532; Fal'tsman, "Intensifikatsiia," 1978, p. 26.

for the reconstruction of these enterprises were very meager. In the post-war years, in the process of rebuilding enterprises destroyed or damaged in the war, all partially damaged foundations and building frames and all walls and other structural elements left intact were used. It was necessary to begin production in a very short period of time, and a large amount of equipment brought from Germany as reparations was installed in existing enterprises in the process.

In the 1950s the attainment of still higher rates of industrial development in conjunction with such massive investment programs as the construction of the Volga-Don canal, the Angaro-Yenisei hydroelectric and industrial complex, and the opening of the virgin lands, to say nothing of the arms programs, intensified the strain in the investment sphere to the limits and made it impossible to allocate sufficient resources for the replacement of worn-out assets. The retirement of fixed capital during these years was the lowest of the entire 50-year period (for which data are available) from 1928 to 1978: in 1951-55, the coefficient of withdrawal of fixed capital in industry was 0.9-1.3.[81] The wear and tear of fixed assets proceeded to such an extent that their use in production was impossible without an unavoidable increase in expenditures on repair. Expenditures on the repair of industrial fixed capital in 1955 were 60 percent higher than in 1951.[82]

In the 1960s the situation did not change; the accumulating needs for replacing fixed assets continued to grow.

The huge and growing scale of replacement in the 1970s, which grew with the expansion of reconstruction, represented a reinvestment echo—a brake on the policies of earlier years. And the effects of these earlier policies bred in the form of the extensive replacement needed were all the greater since so few resources had been spent to maintain and renovate assets in the past.

In examining the effect of reconstruction on the modernization of productive capacity in industry, one other important aspect of the problem must not be forgotten. The replacement of fixed capital that is retired has no independent economic form. It is an abstract category, an accounting value, and not a concrete form embodied in capital investment. We may, of course, also speak of the replacement of a unit of capacity rather than a unit of value.[83] From this standpoint it is correct to view the creation of new enterprises as replacement. Is this path not more efficient from all points of view? Studying the factual

---

[81] Data through 1955: Kvasha, *Amortizatsiia*, 1959, p. 100; since 1956: the yearbooks *Narkhoz* for the corresponding years.
[82] P. Pavlov, *Snashivanie i amortizatsiia osnovnykh fondov*. Moscow: Gosfinizdat, 1957, p. 268.
[83] V. L. Smith, *Investment and Production*. Cambridge, 1961, p. 131.

data characterizing reconstruction and comparing it with analogous indicators for new construction[84] makes it possible to answer this question affirmatively.

The reinvestment cycle in Soviet industry, which began in the 1970s and continues today, is a natural phenomenon that corresponds with economic theory. But because of the cyclical nature of investment processes it should be expected that the peak of replacement, which is natural for a period of declining growth rates of investment, should be supplanted by a growth in the share of net investment, which is characterized by a surge in investment. But the question is: can the onset of a sharp increase in investment be expected in the near future?

Given the realities of contemporary Soviet conditions, this theoretical scheme is upset by the effects of several economic and political factors.

The slowdown in technical progress in producers' goods causes the qualitative level of fixed capital to lag behind its quantitative growth. As a result the growth of the productive potential of fixed capital declines and the accumulation of resources to ensure a rise in investment slows down.

---

[84]L. Bugaets and Z. Parshina, "O snizhenii sebestoimosti produktsii na rekonstruiruemykh i novykh predpriiatiiakh," *Finansy SSSR*, 1978, no. 3, pp. 22, 24.

CHAPTER THREE

INVESTMENT PROBLEMS IN THE 1980s

And so, it is our opinion that the intensification of production and a long-term increase in its efficiency are incompatible with a decrease in investment activity. Only an increase in such activity can serve as the starting point for intensification. The conclusion is being thoroughly confirmed by the development of the economy in the second half of the 1970s.

Prof. Konstantin Val'tukh, 1982

THE MAIN FEATURES OF THE INVESTMENT PROGRAM FOR THE FIRST HALF OF THE 1980s

The investment program for the first half of the 1980s promises to further exacerbate the contradictions and disproportions which arose in industry in the 1970s. The program is distinguished by the following features.

• First—the stabilization of or decrease in investment activity. Capital investments will either be stabilized at 1980 levels (if we believe the report of Minister of Finance Garbuzov at the November, 1981 session of the Supreme Soviet),[1] or else will increase only very slightly (if we follow the version of the plan which s published in the papers).[2]

• The second—the sharp increase in industry's share. Along with the tendency to stabilize capital investments in the national economy as a whole, a significant (23 percent) increase in industrial investment is projected.[3] In this regard, industry's share has grown from 35-36 percent in the increase.[4] Meanwhile, the projected share of agriculture shows a small increase over the 27 percent of the previous period.[5]

At the expense of which branches of the national economy will the increase in industry's investment quota be realized? At the expense of transport? This is a bottleneck in the country's economy,

---

[1] *Pravda*, November 18, 1981.
[2] *Pravda*, November 20, 1981.
[3] See the report on the 11th FYP by Gosplan Chairman N. Baybakov at the November 1981 Supreme Soviet session, in ibid., Nov. 18, 1981.
[4] In the 1970s industry's share was in the vicinity of 35 percent. See *Narkhoz 1980*, pp. 336-337.
[5] *Narkhoz 1980*, pp. 336-337.

and given the growing territorial polarization of the raw-material and fuel industries vis-a-vis the processing industries, the need for transcontinental conveyance has been growing significantly of late. This brings to the fore the need (for additional investments in transport; it would hardly justify a reduction.

As before, it is the non-productive sphere of the economy which will be sacrificed. Garbuzov most definitely talks about this in his report:

> We have resolved that our task is to limit the construction of administrative buildings, entertainment facilities, and sports facilities, as well as structures erected over and above the limits of state capital investments, through noncentralized sources of financing.[6]

Here he is also talking about housing construction, since nearly one-fourth of the new housing built in the '70s was financed through non-centralized capital investments "over and above the limits of state capital investments."

• Third, there is even greater emphasis on renovation, as opposed to construction. At the 26th CPSU Congress, Premier Tikhonov declared:

> In particular, it is necessary to speak about capital investments directed at the reconstruction and technological retooling of existing enterprises .... The task before us consists of even greater application of investments in reconstruction and an increase in its share of overall capital investment.[7]

Although the thesis about the need to increase the share of renovation runs throughout the entire investment section in the 11th five-year plan, one gets the distinct impression from recently published materials that this general idea is provoking resistance among "industrial executives" at every level, and that they are currently impeding its implementation.

Over the whole of the past decade, when renovation was the focus of party and government decrees and propaganda, the share of genuine modernization in industrial investments did not exceed 30 percent. In his speech at the session of the Supreme Soviet, Nikolai Baibakov suggested that this indicator would increase to 32.5 percent between 1981 and 1985. On the other hand, A. Stepun, one of the key people in Soviet investment planning, reports that in the current five-year plan, the share of technological reequipping and modernization will remain

---

[6] *Izvestiya*, Feb. 28, 1981.
[7] *Izvestiya*, Feb. 28, 1981.

practically unchanged, increasing from 29.4 percent to only 29.7 percent.[8]

Let us see what the most authoritative Soviet experts have to say about this. A. Stepun, whom we met above, writes:

> The ministries and industrial associations suppose that it is simpler to "order" a new enterprise from builders and then allege that they have violated the terms of construction, than to bear responsibility for the completion of renovation and technological re-equipping projects. The heads of many enterprises continue to feel that renovation is an irksome task, and somehow less prestigious than new construction.
>
> The ministries did not work out, in time for the eleventh five-year plan, long-term plans for technological re-equipping on the basis of new technology—plans which would have determined the scope and order of priority of work which has to be fulfilled at individual enterprises, and which would give us a clear impression of the economic efficiency of this work vis-a-vis new construction.[9]

P. Ignatovsky, the editor-in-chief of Gosplan's journal *Planovoe khoziaistvo*, in his discussion of "the ratio of capital investments in renovation to investments in new construction," characterizes this question as

> ... a problem permeated with contradictions engendered both by objective conditions and the subjective position of individual departments and the heads of certain enterprises. It is necessary to change the approach of the ministries and planning organs toward renovation. After all, it is no accident that, at present, more and more efforts are being made to receive capital investments for new construction: *the latter better guarantees fixed capital stock, and labor reserves, while putting new objects into operation expands the productive potential of an industry* (emphasis mine—B.R.).[10]

The confrontation between Gosplan and the leaders of industry regarding the distribution of investments between renovation and the construction of new enterprises is intensifying. This is especially borne out by the fact that despite all the restrictions and a drop in capital investments in 1982, the heads of te ministries and the union republics

---

[8]A. Stepun, "O ratsional'nom napravlenii kapital'nykh vlozhenii v odinnadtsatoi pyatiletke," *Planovoe khozyaistvo*, no. 10, 1981, p. 36

[9]A. Stepun, "O ratsional'nom ...," p. 36.

[10]P. Ignatovskii, "Tendentsii ekonomicheskogo razvitiya v 80e gody," *Voprosy ekonomiki*, no. 2, 1981, pp. 79-80.

included in their 1982 investment programs three times more new construction than in the previous year. Gosplan, in turn, cut back sharply on these proposals. But Gosplan doesn't always win: Stepun observes that "... in a number of case, we *had to* (emphasis mine—B.R.) resort to new construction in order to guarantee the assigned levels of production in the current five-year plan, and to create the necessary surpluses for coming years."[11] Later, the author cites the following statistics: in the sume total of capital investments earmarked for production in the 1981 plan, the share of new construction was 50 percent, the share of expansion 31 percent, and the share of reconstruction per se—a mere 19 percent in all.[12] So much for reality.

When summing up his discussion of the five-year plan in his concluding remarks before the Supreme Soviet, Baibakov noted "In their presentations, a number of deputies asked that we provide additional construction of new enterprises and structures in the five-year plan."[13] Judging by the fact that the chairman of Gosplan did not come out positively for these, requests, it is evident that they have not found support among the Soviet leadership.

• The fourth—the extraordinary efforts being made to cut down on uncompleted construction and the concentration of investment resources on a limited number of projects in the final stages of construction. Strictly speaking, this cannot be considered a feature of the investment policy of the current five-year plan, since in Soviet history there has never been a five-year plan which has not proclaimed the need for cutting down on uncompleted construction and concentrating capital investments. Nevertheless, never before did investment dispersion reach such apalling proportions as in the late '70s, when early 80,000 industrial establishments were being built or renovated at the same time.[14] Despite all the efforts of the central leadership to reduce—or at least not to increase— the number of newly started construction projects, they have until now not succeeded in doing so, and the increase in the number of such projects has been as spontaneous as a chain reaction.

Ever-dwindling resources in this rapidly expanding construction galaxy have turned industrial construction into an uncontrollable process. The reduction in investment potentialities dictates the iron necessity to concentrate resources and organizational efforts on those construction projects most vital to the national economy. Judging from the

---

[11] A. Stepun, "O ratsional'nom ...," p. 38.
[12] Op. cit., p. 39.
[13] *Izvestiya*, 20 November 1981, p. 3.
[14] *Metody i praktika opredeleniya effektivnosti kapital'nykh vlozhenii i novoi tekhniki*, No. 32. Moscow: Nauka, 1981, p. 132.

Soviet press, the resolve of the Soviet leadership on this question is attaining hitherto unheard-of proportions.

Three points in Brezhnev's report on the five-year plan at the Central Committee plenum in November, 1981 testify to this:
- a 30-billion-ruble reduction in "the volume of capital investments and construction-installation work originally projected for the five-year plan;"[15]
- an indication of the necessity to take measures to maintain frozen "temporarily discontinued") construction projects;
- concern over establishing construction reserves for the 12th five-year plan, "especially in the raw-material industries."

Concentrating investment activity on a limited number of nearly completed projects must inevitably lead to a reduction in the number of construction projects proper, and to hypertrophy in the volume of equipment assembly and installation.

- Fifth—the eastern regions of the country are now receiving a larger share of new capital than ever before.

Whatever large-scale economic problems may have been solved in Siberia in the Soviet years, its share of the investment pie has never exceeded 17 percent.[16] For a quarter of a century, from 1951 to 1975, it increased by approximately two percentage points: from 15 percent to 17 percent. After 1975, data on the territorial distribution of capital investments disappear from published sources. However, Minas Chentemirov, one of the architects of Soviet investment policy, referring to *Kapital'noe stroitel'stvo v SSSR* (Moscow, 1979), a statistical handbook for 1978 which was never put on sale, reported that Siberia's share in 1978 was 20 percent.[17] Consequently, in three years (from 1976 to 1978) there has been a 3 percent increase.

Such a disturbance in the territorial structure of capital investments—unprecedented for the Soviet Union's inert investment planning—corresponds to an equally dramatic shift in the branch structure of industrial investments: a leap in investments in Siberia's fuel industry, which in the current decade must not only compensate for the falling off in production of the fuel reserves in the European part of the country, but also guarantee their total increment throughout the USSR as a whole.

In the critical period of the war, in 1941, the extremely powerful State Defense Committee, which was headed by Stalin, set up its authorized representatives in the provinces. These SDC representatives

---

[15] *Pravda*, 17 November, 1981, p. 2.

[16] Except for the war years, when Siberia's share increased to 18 percent, because of the fact that industry was evacuated there from the Western regions of the country.

[17] *Metody i praktika* ..., p. 130.

were invested with extraordinary power, and were told to increase arms production at all costs. Forty years later, in 1981, in peace time, the Soviet leadership once again established a corps of authorized representatives, this time for Gosplan. Instead of being sent around to many different regions, these representatives work only in Siberia and the Far East. Their function is guarantee that the Siberian fuel-and-energy program is realized.

Apparently, this decision has been dictated by the realization that Siberia will play the decisive role in rescuing the Soviet economy from the desperate position into which Brezhnev's government has led it.

It turns out that the provincial state and party bureaucracies have been inadequate for realizing the policies of the central leadership and for overcoming the problem of "localism" versus "departmentalism" in carrying out the plan in the vast territories of the East. This will now be the job of special emissaries from the Center.

What is more, efforts to organize and realize the investment programs set up in these regions have led to the creation of an all-union ministry of Siberian construction.

We are thus confronted with remarkable organizational-management decisions which testify to the growing nervousness of the Soviet regime vis-a-vis fulfilling the plans for developing the Siberian economy.

CONSTRUCTION CHALLENGES THE MACHINE-BUILDING INDUSTRY

Naturally, the concentration of new capital on a limited number of nearly-completed projects is an abrupt violation of the investment rhythm which had been established in Soviet industry. Such a spasm cannot but lead to a disturbance in the stratification of industrial construction. Since the main effort is supposed to be directed at partially-completed projects, one should expect a sharp increase in the demand for equipment. Meanwhile, the Soviet machine-building industry is presented with a task that it is not up to.

In the late 1970s, for the first time in Soviet history (excluding the war years), production of most types of metallurgic, metal-working, chemistry-related, and energy-related equipment was curtailed. There was also a reduction in the output of many kinds of equipment intended for the fuel-extraction industries (coalcutters, pipe-borers pumps, machinery for the petroleum industry). But at the same time, the five-year plan stipulates growth in precisely these industries, and more and more investments are being directed toward their accelerated development.

Even more important is the fact that there has been a decline in the number of new productive capacities put into operation in the machine-building industry. The drop in the production of metal, and its low quality, merely aggravate the situation. Therefore, there are no grounds for expecting that the Soviet machine-building industry will be able to deal with such excessive demands—obligations which are arising because of the sharp increase in demand for equipment occasioned by the planned transfer of resources to construction projects in the final stages of completion.

Accelerating the development of the machine-building industry is a process which has major ramifications for the forward development of many other industries, and which, making allowances for time lags, demands a significant period of time.

AMELIORATING FACTORS

It would be a mistake, however, to suppose that the transfer of investment activity from the first stages of construction to the installation and adjustment of equipment will immediately provoke catastrophic shortages of equipment. Two factors will soften this collision.

The first—the reserves of spare equipment—will play an essential, though short-term, role in the beginning of the period. Equipment inventories have been building up for many years in the warehouses of industrial enterprises, construction sites, and material-technological supply organizations.

By no means do industrial enterprises need this whole mass of equipment and spare parts for their normal functioning. This accumulation is predominantly associated with a constantly growing deficit. Under such conditions, enterprises regularly strive to build inventories of equipment for exchange, or merely for a rainy day. It frequently happens that this equipment has nothing to do with the enterprise's technology. Helping to broaden the scope of this phenomenon is the growing tendency to turn enterprises into autarchic units having their own repair centers, building departments, etc. In his report at the 26th CPSU congress, Premier Tikhonov declared: "We cannot accept the fact that many enterprises are hoarding more than their share of equipment, raw materials, and processed materials, while others do not have enough."[18]

Eliminating these extra reserves and then redistributing the equipment is no small task, even for a centralized economy. Nevertheless, it will be possible, apparently, to mobilize a significant portion of these reserves and put them into operation, especially within a given industry. Although this circumstance will not solve the principal problem, it will to a certain extent alleviate the situation, at least within the limits of the current five-year plan.

[18] *Materialy 26 s"ezda KPSS*, Moscow, 1981, p. 126.

The second—the importation of equipment—is of a long-term nature, and its role will seemingly intensify.

It would be natural, given the conditions described above, to increase equipment imports. However, it is no less vitally important to increase imports of agricultural products. So, it is a case of "grain or machines," and here lies the fatal conflict in Soviet import planning, a problem which became especially acute in the early '80s.

In the second half of the 1970s, the percentage of equipment imports in the total volume of Soviet imports changed dramatically. Over the whole 25-year period 1950-75 it increased steadily, growing from 22 percent to 34 percent, but in only three years, between 1976 and 1978, it jumped to 42 percent, only to drop again to 34 percent in the last two years of the decade.[19]

Meanwhile, the percentage of agricultural products was reduced from 23 percent to 19 percent between 1976 and 1978, then once again increased, to 24 percent, in 1980.[20] Agricultural import quotas depend on the nature of the grain harvest: they were reduced in 1976-78, which were years of good harvest, and increased in 1979 and 1980, which saw poor harvests. The correlation between the level of the grain harvests and the volume of equipment imports will be felt in the foreseeable future as well. Thus, the volume of equipment imports to a certain extent depends on the elements.

But the need to transfer foreign-currency reserves to larger and larger purchases of grain, meat, and other agricultural products is not the only thing which has caused a drop in the volume of Soviet equipment imports. Another reason is the increased stockpiling of uninstalled imported equipment (see above), and its low level of utilization due to poor maintenance. Periodic inspections by the investment bank of the USSR and other organizations, which became more frequent toward the end of the 1970s, revealed such facts, and led the Soviet leadership to conclude that it would be expedient to curtail equipment imports for certain industries in this period. But this is a temporary phenomenon, and one should expect the pendulum to swing the other way again shortly.

In the above section, we have been discussing only the importation of machinery from Western countries. But in evaluating the possibilities for providing the Soviet economy with equipment, we must also consider another important factor, a factor of ever-increasing significance—the expanding role of the Comecon countries.

[19] *Narkhoz 1980*, p. 540.
[20] Ibid.

In the latter half of the 1970s, there occurred a shift in the geographical structure of Soviet equipment imports, in the direction of the Comecon countries. This was felt especially strongly in the importation of subsurface and open-pit mining equipment, and equipment for oil refineries. At the same time, Western imports of several other kinds of equipment (e.g., equipment for rolling mills and the chemical industry) increased. without delving deeply into the problem of equipment imports, let us at least draw a cautious conclusion from what has been said: if the Soviet leadership really manages to realize the policy of concentrating investment resources on virtually-completed construction projects which has been incorporated into the five-year plan, and can hold the fort on new construction, then the demand for Western machinery will inevitably increase.

DRAWING CERTAIN ANALOGIES WITH THE PAST

Here it would be appropriate to look into the past. Already once in the postwar period has there been a huge, sudden increase in investment in a particular industry, and this ended in failure. In the early '60s, Khrushchev thought it would be a good idea to dramatically develop "big chemistry;" but the chemical industry was in no position to swallow such a large amount of investment rubles, and wound up choking on them instead. In four years this industry's share of industrial investment increased by almost five percentage points. However, results in the form of an increase in the number of productive capacities put into operation and an increment in output, were totally inadequate, given the extraordinary nature of this investment activity. The basic reason for this is the fact that "big chemistry's" investment program was only 50 percent covered by equipment.[21] Industries closely connected to the chemical industry were not prepared to carry out this program.

At that time, all of the economy's investment proportions were violated, thousands of construction projects were put on hold, and for the first time there appeared surpluses of construction materials and many kinds of equipment. In a word, this action created chaos throughout the investment sphere, and the consequences of this chaos were felt not only throughout the 1960s, but also well into the 1970s. Given the nature of the Soviet economy, one should never (in the words of Victor Krasovsky) "attempt such a sharp turn in the ship of construction."[22] Could the hypertrophied investment program for the

---

[21]V. Krasovsky, *Problemy ekonomiki kapital'nykh vlozhenii.* Moscow: Ekonomika, 1967, p. 17.
[22]Op. cit., p. 4.

Siberian fuel industries be a recurrence of the "big chemistry" fever, and will it not aggravate the drop in Soviet investment potential for a long time?

The fuel-and-energy complex, which involves many different processes such as extraction, transformation, transportation, and the distribution of energy resources, is one of the most capital-intensive spheres of the economy. Directly or indirectly, it uses up nearly 20 percent of all the metal produced in the Soviet Union, and more than 15 percent of the output of the machine-building industry.[23] This is why its development is so very dependent on the resources of those industries which supply it. Increasing the growth rate of the fuel-and-energy industries must entail the accelerated development of many other industries—industries both closely interconnected and far removed—with an allowance for the corresponding time lags.

However, in the late 1970s there was a reduction in the number of capacities put into operation, as well as a drop in output, in all these industries, among others. We have already mentioned the reduction in output of cutters for the coal industry, and pipe-borers, drilling apparatus, and compressors for the oil industry.

Thus, again, only a sharp increase in the importation of machines, other equipment, high-quality steel, etc. can make up for the drop in production, the decreasing number of new capacities, and the inadequacy of investment reserves in those industries which supply the fuel-and-energy complex; and only this will make the fulfillment of the five-year plan for fuel and energy possible.

It is entirely a question of whether or not the Soviet leadership will be able to redistribute import reserves to this end, and whether or not the state of Soviet agriculture will allow this. If not, there is only one alternative left: cut back on the arms program. In the final analysis, it all depends on how one selects one's political priorities.

INVESTMENTS MUST CLIMB FOR INDUSTRIAL OUTPUT TO INTENSIFY

Soviet economists, both theoretical and Gosplan specialists, clearly realize that the sharp curtailment in the increase in capital investment that began in the mid-1970s, which is officially explained by a striving to balance available resources with the scale of construction and thereby create more favorable conditions for economic growth, has not only failed to give the expected results but has still further exacerbated the

---

[23]Yu. Kononov, "Vneshnie proizvodstvennye svyazi i inertsionnost' razvitiya toplivno-energeticheskogo kompleksa," *Izvestiya Sibirskogo otdeleniya Akademii nauk SSSR, seriya obshchestvennykh nauk*, no. 6, vypusk 2, 1981, p. 12.

situation in the investment sphere of the economy.

The investment decline was not a planned economic maneuver. It developed spontaneously and in adapting to it various theoretical concepts were fabricated, which, in particular, include the idea of the universal effectiveness of the reconstruction of existing enterprises and the hypothesis based on Domar's model (even theories of "bourgeois economists" are used when they are needed) of the possibility of expanding production capacities at the expense of depreciation under conditions of declining investment.

Have the hopes of the Soviet leadership that the slowdown in investment would promote improvement in the management of investment processes and, thus, increased effectiveness of investments been realized? If a concentration of investment resources and an appreciable reduction in the amount of unfinished construction had been attained, if the commissionings of production capacities had not lagged farther and farther behind the initiation of investments, if, finally, start-ups of new capacities had accelerated, then we could speak of healthier investment activity in the economy. However, in fact, just the opposite is happening in all respects. As the director of the Research Institute of USSR Gosplan, Vadim Kirichenko, attests:

> Capital investment is being dissipated across an expanding front of construction undertaken simultaneously, and a a result the time required to make investments operational is twice as great as normative construction periods and unfinished construction is about two times larger than its normative magnitude. The cost per unit of capacity commissioned is growing systematically. And this leads to the long-existing imbalance in the sphere of capital construction, to the low effectiveness of the use of the national economic resources channeled there.[24]

In the same publication, Kirichenko reports that commissionings of production capacities are lagging almost 50 percent behind the initiation of new investments. All these data relate to the beginning of the 1980s.

Confusion reigns among theoreticians and practitioners working out investment plans for the second half of the 'eighties. The same Kirichenko writes about this:

> At present (in the period of preparing for the Twelfth Five-Year Plan (1986-1990 B.R.) and determining the directions of economic development for the long term) the need has arisen to define the set of

---

[24] V. Kirichenko, "O nekotorykh voprosakh dal'neishego sovershenstvovaniya planirovaniya i upravleniya khozyaistvom," *Planovoe khozyaistvo*, 1982, no. 9, p. 63.

alternative investment policy possibilities: to maintain the tendency toward a reduction in rates of increase in capital investment or already in the near future to substantiate the need for a certain growth in the dynamics of capital investment, to shift to a regime of increased investment activity. The Twelfth Five-Year Plan period must be the critical period in this respect.

Balance calculations made at the Scientific-Research Economics Institute show that a further slowdown in the rates of growth of capital investment in the next five-year period (even given a certain increase in these rates in the following two five-year periods and rather strained targets for effectiveness) will lead to a reduction in the growth rates of national income in the 1990s to an annual average level of 3 percent and less and to an even more appreciable reduction in the growth of the consumption fund than in preceding periods. If we propose a certain acceleration in rates of growth of investment—by about 1.5 percentage points beginning in the Twelfth Five-Year Plan and by 2-3 points in each of the following five-year periods—then we can expect to overcome the tendency toward a reduction in the rates of growth of national income, to ensure their stable acceleration in the 1990s, to significantly increase nonproductive capital investments, and to achieve stable growth of current consumption and the population's real incomes. Expanding resources for nonproductive consumption will also make it possible to implement a more active social policy. Carrying out this variant will require an increase in the share of investment in machine building, the construction materials industry, construction, and also the chemical industry.

Thus, it appears especially important to seek possibilities and reserves for changing the existing trend in the dynamics of capital investment already in the Twelfth Five-Year Plan, of course to the extent permitted by objective resource possibilities.[25]

Thus, the director of one of the leading scientific economic centers informing theoretical concepts of Soviet economic planning asserts on the basis of research carried out that overcoming the decline in national income is possible only with an increase in the rate of growth of investment—that plans for the development of the Soviet economy in the second half of the 1980s should be based on a rising investment curve. It follows that the course of intensifying the use of investment, which was widely promoted in the Soviet economic literature and which was the essence, the core of the economic doctrine of the Soviet leadership since the end of the 1960s, has failed.

---

[25] Ibid., p. 62.

THE RESTRUCTURING OF INDUSTRIAL INVESTMENTS: THE FIRST AND FOREMOST CONDITION FOR INDUSTRIAL GROWTH

Specifically, Kirichenko notes the need to increase the investment quota of machine building, which has almost stabilized in recent years. The same thing is emphasized by another, no less authoritative, Soviet scholar, Academician Vadim Trapeznikov, who sees underinvestment in machine building as precisely the basic reason for the insufficient development of technical progress in the USSR.[26] Thus, following the opinion of these two eminent Soviet experts, reviving investment activity hinges first of all on a restructuring of investment in favor of machine building, in shifting to that branch of the economy substantially greater resources than has been the case to date. Can we expect this idea to be implemented in the foreseeable future? To evaluate the real possibilities of restructuring the branch distribution of industrial investment in the direction of an increased share for machine building, we must examine at least briefly the following fundamental structural factor that determines the most important parameters of the investment process in Soviet industry, including the distribution of investment among branches of the economy and regions of the country. Raw materials, fuel, and basic industrial materials (metal, cement, etc.) account for more than half of the gross social product of the USSR. Their production consumes up to 40 percent of all productive capital and labor resources and about 30 percent of capital investment in the economy.[27]

During 1950-80 the share of production of raw materials, fuel, and primary processed materials in the total volume of Soviet industrial production increased from 51 percent to 59 percent, and the share of products of the manufacturing industry decreased correspondingly from 49 percent to 41percent (in current prices).[28]

We see the following explanations for this important trend in the Soviet economy. The first objective factor is the orientation of the economy of the USSR toward its own natural resources. The USSR occupies first or one of the first places the world in reserves of a whole series of the most important types of mineral resources and the volume of their extraction. The USSR almost fully satisfies its needs from its own mineral resources. And the growth rates of extraction of mineral resources in the USSR exceed world growth. This is confirmed by the following data which show the extraction of mineral resources during 1951-80 relative to total extraction for a period over 100 years (in %)

---

[26] *Pravda*, May 7, 1982.
[27] I. Pasko, "Rezervy snizheniya materialoemrosti," *EKO*, 1976, no. 3, p. 32.
[28] "Promyshlennost' SSSR," Statistika, Moskva, 1957, p. 13. *Narkhoz 1980*, p. 124.

TABLE 3

EXTRACTION OF MINERAL RESOURCES[29]

	1951-1980 as % of 1876-1980	
	world extraction	extraction in USSR
Coal	54.4	81.9
Oil	85.6	90.5
Natural gas	89.2	98.6
Iron ore	64.4	87.6

While in 1926-50 the share of the USSR in world extraction of coal was 8.5 percent, in 1976-80 it was 15.8 percent; corresponding figures for oil are 8.3 percent and 19.3 percent, natural gas 2.6 percent and 23.5 percent, and iron ore 9.8 percent and 28.9 percent.[30]

But maintaining and increasing the rates of extraction of raw materials and fuel, not only to satisfy growing domestic needs but for increasing exports, consumes ever greater capital resources. The production of raw materials and fuel is much more capital intensive than their processing. According to contemporary Soviet data, capital investments in creating capacities for the annual production of one million rubles of raw materials and fuel amount to about 4 million rubles, and in creating capacities for their processing—0.7 million. On the average for all raw materials branches the additional annual production of 1 ruble of raw materials required capital expenditures of 2 rubles in 1960, 3 rubles in 1970, and about 4 rubles in 1980.[31] Soviet economists forsee still further growth in the future. Expenditures on geological-prospecting work are increasing by 10-15 percent annually.[32] And here we may note that in the extent of geological exploration the USSR occupies one of the last places among developed countries of the world. Even with the huge scale of production of oil and gas in West Siberia, with the tremendous proved reserves of coal, systematic exploratory work in Siberia is only just beginning.

[29]N. Feitel'man, "Mineral'no-syr'evaya baza SSSR," *Voprosy ekonomiki*, 1982, no. 12, p. 60.
[30]Ibid., p. 61.
[31]Ibid., p. 65.
[32]Ibid.

The increase in expenditures on the production of raw materials and fuel is due not only the growth of the scale of production, but to the poorer quality of many types of minerals obtained from the deposits that are exploited. Let us take, as an example, ferrous metallurgy.

Unlike the metallurgical industries of other industrially developed countries, Soviet metallurgy uses its own deposits of iron ore, not resorting to imports. While having over 50 percent of world reserves of iron ore, the USSR uses ores that are less rich in comparison with other industrially developed countries and extracts them with significantly greater and continuously growing costs. The iron content of raw ore on the average in the USSR was 50 percent in 1950, and 35 percent in 1980. As a result, the share of ore undergoing enrichment increased during this period from 37 percent to 87 percent, which, in turn, led to a sharp increase in capital expenditures (they were, in constant prices, 61 rubles per ton in 1966-70 and 102 rubles per ton in 1976-80).[33] We must also consider the huge scale of ore shipments. Thus, a metallurgical plant located in the region of the Kursk-Magnitogorsk Anomaly receives Kuznets Basin coking coal shipped a distance of 3,000 kilometers by rail. Maintaining and developing the mining complex is made still more difficult to the extent that deposits in inhabited regions are exhausted and it is necessary to shift to developing deposits indistant regions of the north and northeast with an undeveloped infrastructure.

A second factor, though not of an objective nature, is the low technological level of the processing of raw materials in the USSR and hence the low quality of the materials themselves which leads to increases in their consumption. We will continue to use metallurgy as an example.

Per ruble of national income, 50 percent more metal is used in the USSR than in the U.S.,[34] which is explained primarily by the lag in the technology of metalworking. The USSR produces more steel than the U.S. (42 percent more in 1980) but produces approximately 30-40 percent less machine-building output. Soviet machinery and equipment is on the average 25 percent more metal intensive than American.[35] Thus, the consumption of raw materials in the USSR proceeds on a scale and at rates exceeding the growth of production of final industrial output.

The same is true of fuel-energy resources, and in this case a large role is played by the existing proportions of energy sources in providing for final consumption of energy. To say nothing of the fact that

---

[33] A. Tselikov, "Ekonomiya metallov pri novoi tekhnologii," *Planovoe khozaistvo*, 1979, no. 8, p. 56.
[34] I. Pashko, "Rezervy ...," p. 32.
[35] Based on data for the Ukraine. *EKO*, 1982, no. 12, p. 54.

electricity as an energy source is best suited or implementing modern technology (using higher pressures, accelerating technological cycles and chemical reactions, employing electro-physical methods of metalworking, etc.), it is also the most efficient energy source from the standpoint of consuming mineral fuel. In this sense pay special attention to the following negative trend: in 1950-70 the annual average rate of growth of electricity consumption in the USSR exceeded the rate for the consumption of all fuel-energy resources by 80 percent. In 1971-75 this figure declined to 35 percent and in 1976-80 it amounted to about 15-20 percent. At the same time in industrially developed countries this indicator has for a long time been maintained at a level of 70-100 percent.[36] In the mid-1970s the share of electricity in final energy consumption for the USSR as a whole did not exceed 11-14 percent. Overcoming this trend, i.e., increasing the role of electricity as an energy source, is a necessary condition for optimizing (and reducing) expenditures of mineral fuel.

The increasing overburdening of the economy with the production of raw materials, fuel, and primary processed materials (metal, cement, etc.) leads not only to maintaining their extremely high share in the total volume of industrial production but to expanding it.

Thus, the predominance in industrial production of the extractive complex and industry of the early stages of processing, which is inherent to the Soviet economy, tends to intensify in spite of all efforts of the Soviet leadership to overcome this tendency or at least to check its development. This may be appropriately labeled the primitivization of industrial production in the USSR. But it is not only that the share of machine building in the distribution of investment resources is declining. It is also that the machine-building capacities, exclusive of military production, are to an ever greater extent occupied in satisfying the requirements of the lower stage of industry, and less and less remains for the upper. Less than 10 percent of machine-building output remains for the direct consumption of the population.[37]

A vicious circle has been created: the more resources that are diverted to maintain and develop the production of raw materials, fuels and basic industrial materials, the less that are allocated for the development of technology and the production of equipment; and the more technology lags, the greater the amount of raw materials, fuel, and basic industrial materials that is expended per unit of output—the more the requirements for their production grow. And regardless of

---

[36] "Sibir' v edinom narodnokhozyaystvennom komplekse," Nauka, Novosibirsk, 1980, p. 134.
[37] I. Pashko, "Rezervy ...," p. 32.

how much fuel, metal, and cement is produced, the gap between production and requirements does not shrink but grows. And instances of plants being idled due to the lack of raw materials, fuel, and metal become more frequent. And construction stops due to the lack of cement. This is precisely why in his first "state of the union" address Andropov singled out among the main problems "the lack of integration in the development of raw materials and processing branches" and emphasized that "the material intensiveness of production is not declining."[38]

The exponential expansion of the fuels-raw materials complex to an ever greater extent diverts resources from the quantitative and qualitative development of the economy's machine-building base. In this case, implementing an ambitious investment program is possible only with an increase in imports of equipment and technology, which, in turn, requires an increase in the production of raw materials and fuel for export.

* * * * *

As is well-known, national income—the part allocated for capital accumulation—is the basic source of investment in the Soviet economy. Increases in national income are becoming smaller. The share of accumulation is declining or at least not increasing (the Soviet leadership would hardly allow themselves a further curtailment of consumption). Thus of investment are drying up and all that can be counted on is an in the effectiveness of their use. But the methods chosen lead to the opposite result.

Raising the effectiveness of investment in Soviet industry investment resources that are growing more scarce, requires changing branch and regional investment proportions. Concretely, this means injection of investment in machine building, optimizing the correlation of investments in the development of existing enterprises and the construction of new ones, and also not only increasing the investment share of eastern regions of the country but intensifying investment in manufacturing industry and the construction base in these regions. Carrying out such a reversal is impossible if existing priorities in internal and external policy are retained and the system of planning and economic management remains unchanged.

* * * * *

[38]"Pravda," 23 1982, pp. 1, 2.

changes in the investment process in Soviet industry as a whole. But for the Soviet economy what are becoming more and more important, more and more urgent, are investment decisions which are aimed at overcoming the rapidly widening territorial disproportion in industrial development—the concentration of fuel and raw-material production in the East, and processing and manufacturing in the West. The following chapters of the present monograph are devoted to this extremely important question. In examining them, we have focused our attention on Siberia—especially western Siberia—as the center of investment activity in the Asiatic part of the Soviet Union.

In analyzing the results of the implementation of Siberia's huge investment programs, we considered it expedient to go beyond the bounds of a purely investment-oriented approach and examined certain crucial phenomena which are of enormous significance for the economic development not only of Siberia, but also for the country as a whole.

CHAPTER FOUR

THE EAST'S SHARE OF THE INVESTMENT PIE AND THE ROLE OF SIBERIAN INDUSTRY

The ministry lost its strategy for developing the industry. From the point of view of today's planners, the idea for the Uralo-Kuznetsk combine wouldn't work. They'd consider it inefficient. Efficient for them would be an orientation toward the southern Ural region: there was a construction base there, manpower, a railroad, a lot of ore. But no, then it was into the swamp to build a city, to build a railroad. Colossal funds were needed. There were people opposed to such a decision. But then the idea of greater profitability was put forward. Under this flag there occurred many changes and actions which to other contemporary economists seem inexplicable. Now it is hard to imagine building a city like Komsomolsk-na-Amure in the taiga just to accommodate one plant. Planners now approach things somehow from a utilitarian viewpoint: we'll get a blast furnace here, a mill there, save a million here. But meanwhile many regions in Siberia and the Far East have been put in a difficult position ....

Academician Abel Aganbegian, 1978

For the USSR, a country with extremely great climatic, geographic, and socio-economic differences, the regional aspect of economic development, in general, and investment, in particular, is of great significance. Overcoming the spatial gap between the basic concentrations of economic resources is a necessary condition for the effective functioning of its economy. The main spatial direction for solving this problem is the East-West geographical axis.

The West (the European part and the Urals) accounts for 25 percent of the area of the country and 76 percent of the total population; nearly four-fifths of all fixed capital is concentrated there, and more than four-fifths of gross industrial output and three-fourths of gross agricultural output is produced there. At the same time, by far the largest part of the natural resources is concentrated in the Asiatic part (Siberia, the Far East, Kazakhstan, and Central Asia), which is much less developed economically. Within the Asiatic part, a particularly important role is played by Siberia and the Far East—regions which are very rich in natural resources but which are experiencing huge demands for labor resources.

TABLE 4

COMPARATIVE ECONOMIC CHARACTERISTICS OF THE EUROPEAN AND ASIATIC MACROZONES OF THE USSR (USSR = 100)[1]

Indicator	European	Asiatic Part				
		Total	Siberia	Far East	Kazakh-stan	Central Asia
Area	25	75	25	28	12	6
Population	78	22	5	2	6	9
Energy Resources						
potential	9	91	60	28	2	1
proven	27	73	67	7.5	6	2.5

The acceleration of economic, and above all industrial, development of the eastern regions was one of the main strategic tasks of economic policy of the USSR from the very beginning of its existence. Therefore, a central question in analyzing the regional aspect of the investment process is the trend of redistribution of capital investment from the West to the East and the study of factors contributing to this trend.

In this respect it is important to establish the extent to which the investment activity of the Soviet state was really oriented toward priority development of the Asiatic part of the country: what was the mechanism of spatial distribution of capital investment, and how did it work to ensure the attainment of established goals? Were these goals achieved? What are the likely trends in the regional structure of capital investment in the immediate future?

GENERAL PATTERNS OF CHANGE IN THE SPATIAL STRUCTURE OF CAPITAL INVESTMENT

The data presented in Table 5 provide a basis for judging how the spatial orientation of investment flows changed during the entire Soviet period through 1975.

For the period as a whole there is a weak trend toward an increase in the share of the Asiatic part of the USSR. However, at the end of the period (1971-75), this trend is curtailed and, moreover, a certain inclination to reverse this direction emerges—the share of the European

---

[1]V. A. Shelest, *Regional'nye energo-ekonomicheskie problemy SSSR*, Moscow: Nauka, 1975, pp. 196-197. The figures are as they appear in the book.

part begins to increase somewhat. Throughout this period, the share of the Asiatic macrozone in total capital investment did not once exceed 30 percent.

Deviations from this basic trend require special explanations. During the period in question, there were fundamental changes in both the domestic and foreign policies of the Soviet government, which had a decisive influence on the country's economic development, including investment strategy and tactics. One of the most significant events in this regard was the Second World War.

In analyzing the entire period, 1918-75, it is useful to distinguish the following four subperiods: reconstruction (1918-28), pre-war (1928/29-June, 1941), war (1941-45), and post-war (1946-75). Within the post-war subperiod, we may also distinguish the years of reconstruction of war damage (1946-50) and the Sovnarkhoz period (1957-65). In our opinion, there were qualitatively new features determining the regional structure of investment in the 1970s, and their effect on the investment process will continue to emerge in the 1980s.

The relatively high share of the Asiatic macrozone as a whole during the reconstruction period (1918-28) can be explained by the efforts of the Soviet government to consolidate the outlying districts in the process of forming the USSR, and by the economic stimulation of this process in these regions. The rulers of each republic considered industrialization as a catchword as a necessity for the universal development of their own economy, and the theory of the closed economy for a republic was advanced. Such a position was taken, for example, by the government of Kazakhstan, whose share of capital investment in the country in those years was about 6 percent—quite a bit higher than in all subsequent years until the sharp increase connected with the opening of the Virgin Lands.

The situation changed with the beginning of the first Five-Year Plans. First, the central rulers were already sufficiently powerful to overcome the emergence of autarchic tendencies in various areas. The so-called "nationalist-deviants" were crushed in all republics, and the principle of centralized development of the Soviet economy triumphed fully.

Secondly, the industrialization of the Asiatic part of the country objectively required an "industrial head-start" for the more developed European macrozone. Therefore, investment branches of industry in the European regions (those creating basic fixed assets) received priority in the distribution of capital investment in the years of the first two Five-Year Plans (1928/29-1932 and 1933-37), and the share of the Asiatic macrozone declined significantly.

TABLE 5

SHIFTS IN THE REGIONAL DISTRIBUTION OF USSR AS A WHOLE (PRICES

Region	1918-28 (excl. 4th qtr.)	1928/29 -1932	1933-37	1938- June, 1941	June, 1941- 1945
European macrozone (incl. the Urals)	75.9	79.4	79.5	77.6	73.3
Asiatic macrozone	24.1	20.6	20.5	22.4	26.7
including:					
Eastern zone (Far East and Siberia)	14.8	13.5	13.3	15.0	18.0
of which:					
West Siberia	3.9	4.4	4.0	3.7	6.1
East Siberia	4.5	4.2	3.5	3.8	4.1
Far East	6.3	4.8	5.7	7.6	7.8
Southeastern zone	9.3	7.1	7.2	7.4	8.7
of which:					
Kazakhstan	5.8	3.3	3.4	3.5	4.7
Uzbekistan	1.8	2.0	2.1	2.1	2.3
Tadzhikistan	0.9	0.9	0.6	0.6	0.4
Turkmenistan	0.5	0.6	0.6	0.6	0.7
Kirgizstan	0.4	0.3	0.4	0.8	0.6

[2]An insignificant part of capital investments during 1946-59 and 1951-56 was not distributed among macrozones in the sources used. Data are for capital investment of state and cooperative enterprises and organizations (excluding collective farms) for all periods, except 1971-75, for which collective farms are included.

Data for Siberia in 1966-70 were divided into West and East Siberia using data from *Narkhoz RSFSR 1970*, p. 320. Data for Siberia as a whole were taken from *Problemy teorii i praktiki razmeshcheniia proizvoditel'nykh sil SSSR*. Moscow, Nauka, 1976, p. 83.

Before 1964, Tyumen oblast was a part of the Ural economic region. Since 1965 it has been part of the West Siberian region.

For Turkmenistan, figures for 1940, 1965, 1970, and 1975 were taken from *Narkhoz* handbooks. All other years were calculated by extrapolation.

All other data are from *Narkhoz* handbooks for the USSR, RSFSR, Kazakhstan, Uzbekistan, Tadzhikistan, Turkmenistan, and Kirghizstan, and from M. B. Mazanova, "Territorial'nye proportsii razvitiia proizvoditel'nykh sil strany," in *Problemy*, 1976, p. 83.

CAPITAL INVESTMENT AS A PERCENTAGE OF THE
COMPARABLE WITHIN PERIODS)

1946-50	1951-55	1956-60	1961-65	1966-70	1971-75
79.4	76	74	71.4	70.0	70.9
20.6	24	26	28.6	30.0	29.1
13.0	15.2	15.7	15.7	16.3	16.2
4.4	5.7	6.2	5.9	6.5	7.1
4.1	4.8	5.6	5.4	5.1	4.6
4.5	4.8	3.9	4.4	4.7	4.5
7.4	8.7	10.3	12.9	13.7	12.9
3.7	4.8	6.4	7.6	7.4	6.8
1.9	1.8	2.0	3.0	4.0	3.8
0.5	0.6	0.6	0.7	0.8	0.8
0.8	0.8	0.7	0.8	0.8	0.8
0.5	0.7	0.6	0.8	0.9	0.7

The opposite pattern of two regions within the Asiatic macrozone—West Siberia and the Far East—stands out against the background of this general trend. A decisive feature of investment activity in West Siberia in the 1930s was the construction of the Ural-Kuznets Combine, which accounted for 35.6 percent of all capital investment in industry in Siberia during the First Five-Year Plan.[3]

In the Second Five-Year Plan, there was an increase in investment activity in the Far East, which is explained by the growing tensions in relations between the USSR and Japan and the resulting forced efforts to strengthen the military potential of the Far East. In 1940 this region accounted for 9.5 percent of all fixed capital put into operation (excluding collective farms), while the share of Siberia was 8.8 percent.[4] Never, neither before nor after this period, did the Far East occupy such a dominant position in Soviet investment policy. The share of eastern regions is rising precisely for this reason. The share of Siberia, Kazakhstan, and Central Asia changed little during this entire 30-year period.

A sharp reorientation of the entire regional structure of investment took place during the war years (1941-45) as a result of the relocation of the country's military-industrial base to the eastern regions. Investment shares increased during these years in the Eastern regions (primarily due to West Siberia and Kazakhstan). During the war years, average annual capital investment increased by 23 percent in West Siberia,[5] while at the same time it declined in East Siberia and the Far East.

The significant decline in the share of Eastern regions during the first post-war five-year period is explained by the necessity of shifting investment resources for the reconstruction of war damage to the economy of the European part of the country. (The industry of Eastern regions did not suffer from military actions.)

The share of the Eastern part of the country in the spatial allocation of capital investment grew during the entire post-war period through the beginning of the 1970s.

Post-war investment activity in Siberia was governed by the implementation of three major comprehensive investment programs—the creation of the Angara-Yenisei complex, the development of the oil and gas fields of West Siberia, and the construction of the Baikal-Amur Mainline and economic development of areas adjacent to it.

---

[3] A. S. Moskovskii, *Formirovanie i razvitie rabochego klassa Sibiri v period stroitel'stva sotsializma*. Novosibirsk, 1968, pp. 28-29.
[4] Calculated from data in *Narkhoz SSSR 1967*, p. 607.
[5] *Istoriia Sibiri*, vol. V, Leningrad, 1968, p. 89.

With respect to the Far East, investment activity slowed in the 1950s with the disappearance of the military threat from Japan, but was activated anew with the spread of the conflict with China in the 1960s and 1970s. During the entire period, 1950-75, the share of the Eastern regions remained almost stable (an increase of only one percentage point).

The most significant factor in the increase of the Southeastern zone was the redistribution of capital investment in favor of Kazakhstan in connection with the development of the Virgin Lands, which began in March and April of 1954 and continued through the entire Khrushchev era. Another notable phenomenon is the two-fold increase in the share of Uzbekistan during the 1960s. Of importance here was the intensification of irrigation construction in the Syr Daria and Amu Daria river basins and the growth of extraction and processing of rare nonferous metals in the republic. But the most significant factor was the development of the natural gas industry in Uzbekistan, which began in the early 1960s.

For the other Central Asian republics (Turkmenistan, Tajikistan, and Kirghizstan), whose combined share of investment did not exceed 2.5 percent, the extent of their participation in the spatial allocation of capital investment remained essentially unchanged.

The data in Table 6 were calculated to check the conclusions outlined above. Therefore, not only investment but other characteristics of the investment process were included—fixed capital installed and the volume of construction-installation work. For a further analysis, the Eastern regions are compared not with the entire European USSR, but only with a group of the most industrially developed regions the Northwest, Central, Volga, Don-Pridnepr, and Ural economic regions, which are historically the industrial nucleus of Russia.

Table 6 shows that the share of regions grouped as zone 1 in total national capital investment declined substantially (by almost 11 percentage points) during the period considered, which certainly represents an appreciable shift in the spatial structure of investment. But during this period the share of regions in the other two zones (that is, the entire Asiatic macrozone) increased by only 2.7 percentage points. The share of the Eastern zone remained unchanged, although there was a slight increase at times during the period. An analysis of the data of Table 6 leads to the conclusion that first, the share of regions in the first group (the industrial nucleus) remains high in spite of a decline, and secondly, the decline in the share of this group was halted in the 1970s, and the overall spatial structure of capital investment in the country stabilized. Data on fixed capital installed and the volume of construction-installation work support these conclusions.

TABLE 6

TRENDS IN INDICATORS CHARACTERIZING SPATIAL SHIFTS IN INVESTMENT (AS A PERCENTAGE OF THE USSR AS A WHOLE)[6]

Year	Capital Investment Zone 1	2	3	Fixed Capital Installed Zone 1	2	3	Construction-Installation Work Zone 1	2	3
1958	50.3	10.2	15.7	52.4	9.7	15.0	51.3	10.0	15.3
1959	47.0	10.3	16.0	50.2	10.1	15.0	48.1	10.3	16.4
1960	46.9	11.4	16.6	47.6	12.2	14.7	47.0	11.2	16.4
1961	44.7	12.4	16.1	46.0	12.6	16.4	45.6	12.4	16.4
1962	44.4	12.4	16.0	45.6	12.1	16.5	45.2	12.8	16.7
1963	43.6	12.7	16.0	45.6	12.3	16.7	44.3	13.3	16.9
1964	44.2	13.3	16.1	45.1	12.7	15.6	44.1	13.5	16.6
1965	43.6	13.8	16.0	43.7	13.6	15.9	43.5	14.2	16.5
1966	—	14.0	—	43.6	11.7	15.5	—	14.6	—
1967	—	13.9	—	42.4	11.9	16.7	—	14.6	—
1968	—	13.4	—	43.1	10.8	16.9	—	14.1	—
1969	41.7	11.4	16.4	43.0	11.2	16.2	41.5	11.2	16.8
1970	41.8	13.3	16.5	42.6	13.3	15.8	41.1	14.2	16.9
1971	39.4	12.8	15.7	41.6	13.3	16.8	41.3	13.7	17.1
1972	39.7	12.7	15.8	42.0	13.1	16.5	41.3	13.9	17.4
1973	39.6	12.8	15.9	41.2	13.2	17.1	41.2	14.0	17.5
1974	39.5	12.7	16.1	42.0	13.0	16.9	41.1	14.0	17.5
1975	39.6	12.3	16.8	42.0	12.7	17.3	41.3	13.7	18.0

[6]Zone 1 includes the Northwest, Central, Volga, Don-Pridnepr, and Ural economic regions (according to the existing scheme of regionalization used in the USSR). Zone 2 includes Kazakhstan and the Central Asian economic region. Zone 3 includes the West Siberian, East Siberian, and Far East regions. Source: *Narkhoz RSFSR 1965*, pp. 369, 374, 377, 539. *Narkhoz RSFSR 1970*, pp. 318, 320, 324, 488. *Narkhoz UkSSR 1964*, pp. 414, 415, 422, 423, 426, 427. *Narkhoz UkSSR 1965*, pp. 436, 442, 44. *Narkhoz SSSR 1965*, p. 539. *Narkhoz SSSR 1970*, p. 488. *Narkhoz SSSR 1975*, p. 513.

Thus, did the investment policy of the USSR stimulate a reorientation of industrial development from West to East to any signfiicant extent? During the entire period, 1918-75, there was no sharp change in the spatial distribution of capital investment in favor of the eastern regions. The increase of five percentage points in the share of the Asiatic part of the USSR in capital investment during this period is not evidence of an investment effort sufficient to overcome the intertia in the territorial location of industrial production in the USSR.

What are the results of such an investment policy? Is the spatial redistribution of industrial production from West to East stepped up, and is the structure of industry in the Asiatic part improved? These questions can be answered on the basis of the data in Table 7.

TABLE 7

SHARES OF THE EUROPEAN AND ASIATIC PARTS IN
INDUSTRIAL OUTPUT IN THE LATE '70s
(IN PERCENT)[7]

Branch	European	Asiatic
All Industry	81	19
Electric power	75	25
Fuel	66.8	33.2
Chemical and petrochemical	86.9	13.1
Machine-building and metalworking	86.3	13.7
Timber and woodworking	72.7	27.8
Construction materials	75.0	25.0
Light industry	81.1	18.9
Food	81.3	18.7
Other	85.8	14.2

One of the focal points of the planned development of Soviet industry was the improvement of its spatial proportions, the industrial development of the Eastern regions of the country, and the spatial deconcentration of industrial production. The fact that during almost 60 years the share of the entire Asiatic part, with its basic fuel-energy

[7]L. I. Gramoteeva, *Effektivnost' territorial'noi organizatsiia proizvodstva*. Moscow: Mysl', 1979, p. 155.

and raw material potential, reached only 19 percent of the nation's industrial production indicates that the stated goal was not achieved.

THE FUNDAMENTAL REASONS FOR THE SLOW INVESTMENT FLOW INTO THE EAST

What is standing in the way of a more decisive reorientation of investment flows from the West to the East in order to eliminate the growing disproportion in the regional distribution of industry? Two factors are hindering more rapid shift of manufacturing industry to the East.

First is the emphasis of capital investment on reconstruction under conditions of sharply declining investment activity in the country as a whole. The orientation toward investing in existing enterprises rather than creating new ones results in the existing regional distribution of capital investments being maintained. The reconstruction of industry in the European part of the USSR, which produces 80 percent of the country's industrial output, absorbs a corresponding share of national capital investment.

No more than 7 percent of capital investment in the development of machine-building in the USSR in 1971-75 was in the Eastern regions. The overwhelming share of this investment went for the renovation of plants in the European regions. During the period 1965-75, the share of the Asiatic regions in total machine-building output in the country declined by 3.3 percentage points, and the share of the European region increased by a corresponding amount.[8]

The development of the chemical and petrochemical industry of the USSR is also proceeding along the path of renovation, expansion, and modernization of existing enterprises, primarily in the European regions. Precisely for this reason the share of the Eastern part of the country in the national output of this branch declined from 15.1 to 13.1 percent during 1965-75.[9]

The increase in the share of renovation in industrial capital investment in the USSR contributes to the increase in the share of the European macrozone in the regional distribution of capital investment

The second factor is the domination of the branch principle of planning and management of the economy and the subordination of investment planning to this principle. Let us consider this factor in more detail.

[8]Ibid., pp. 141-143.
[9]Ibid., p. 140.

Soviet economic theory distinguishes two basic principles for the organization of the economy and, correspondingly, two basic principles for constructing the system of economic planning: branch and territorial. The ultimate goal of planning was formulated back in 1920 in a resolution of the Ninth Party Congress: "The organizational problem is to maintain and develop vertical centralization along the lines of the departments while combining it with the horizontal coordination of enterprises along the lines of economic regions, where enterprises of different branches of industry and different economic significance must share one and the same sources of local raw materials, transportation facilities, labor, etc."[10]

Already in the first long-range plan of economic development of the USSR (GOELRO), worked out in 1920, the idea of forming the country's economy not in "individual links" but in "economically independent regional units" was postulated. This principle governed economic planning in the 1920s and the early 1930s. The first five-year plan was elaborated with a regional breakdown. In it emphasis was placed on the comprehensive development of the economy of each region. The idea of the functional completeness and internal stability of regions of various sizes was emphasized. At the end of the second five-year plan, in the middle of the 1930s, when the process of the specialization and centralization of industry began, these ideas faded somewhat. Nonetheless, even in the third five-year plan notable attention was given to the balanced development of the economies of regions. But, by the end of the 1930s, the contradictions between regional and branch interests in economic planning became more severe and were especially noticeable whenever decisions on some economic question regarding the less-developed Eastern regions had to be made. Some Soviet economists pressed for the observance of the comprehensive territorial approach in economic strategy. But as the number of branch ministries multiplied, and as the functions of administration and planning in all spheres of the national economy were transferred to them, the branch principle became dominant.

The realization of the idea of a harmonious combination of branch and regional planning turned out to be impossible. There has been an antagonism between the regional and branch principles of administering and organizing industry that is inherent in the Soviet economy. Excessive manifestations of the territorial principle ("localism" in Soviet political jargon) are, as a rule, suppressed more severely than hypertrophy of the idea of the centralized branch planning and functioning of

---

[10] *KPSS v rezoliutsiiakh i resheniiakh s"ezdov, konferentsii i plenumov TsK.*, vol. 2, eighth ed., 1970, p. 155.

the economy. With the exception of the Sovnarkhoz period (1957-65), which was discussed above, harsh and all-encompassing centralism has ruled the planning of the economy. The interests of comprehensive economic development are ignored not only in oblasts, krais, and the economic regions that exist more in theory, but in union republics. This tendency became especially clear in the second half of the 1940s and the beginning of the 1950s. In directives for the Fifth Five-Year Plan, 1951-55, adopted by the Nineteenth Party Congress, there was not even a separate section for union republics.[11] Targets for the spatial location of production were included only in the branch sections of the plan. The extreme degree of centralization of the control of the economy in ministries was also evident in the elaboration of annual plans, which also had neither sections nor individual indicators for the comprehensive development of the economies of republics. The share of industry subordinated to union republics in 1953 was 31 percent, and republics directly allocated only 5 percent of total national capital investment.[12] All other capital investment was allocated by union ministries, and they considered local interests only after all other factors and then only to the extent necessary for the proper functioning of all-union production facilities.

In the mid-1950s tendencies toward decentralization of administration and planning began to appear, and they led to the complete transfer to the regional principle of economic administration in 1957. In 1961, 93 percent of industry was under the direction of union republics, and they controlled 77 percent of capital investment.[13] Republic Gosplans carried out all long-term and current planning for their territories. The directives for the Sixth Five-Year Plan adopted by the Twentieth Party Congress included an entire section on the development of the economies of republics and, for the first time in the post-war period, on the location of production.[14] But in 1965 the economy of the USSR was returned to the branch principle and ministries were reestablished. At the same time an attempt was made to find the optimal correlation between the branch and territorial principles of economic planning. With respect to investment planning, republics continued to compile capital investment plans but only for enterprises subordinate to them, although they were also to participate in the preparation of plans for all-union industries located within their boundaries.

---

[11]Ibid., vol. 6, 1971, pp. 342-366.
[12]M. S. Urinson, *Planirovanie narodnogo khoziaistva v soiuznykh respublikakh.* Moscow: Ekonomizdat, 1963, pp. 60, 84.
[13]Ibid., p. 65.
[14]*KPSS v rezoliutsiiakh*, vol. 7, pp. 115-181.

However, in most cases the participation of the planning commissions of union republics in the formation of capital investment plans of union ministries is actually purely formal. They merely sum up the various branch plans and projections worked out by ministries. Republic planning commissions retain rudimentary regional planning bodies, which are dependent on branch planning organs for the information they need. All concrete preliminary calculations and estimates are made by branch scientific and design institutes subordinate to branch ministries, and the proposals of regional planning bodies can be based only on these estimates. This, of course, limits the possibilities of local economic planning and administrative organs to influence the development of their republic or region in a particular direction.

In the 1970s the branch basis of all links of the economy was strengthened, including the planning of capital investment. True, the disregard for the comprehensive development of republics, individual regions, and oblasts is not as blatant as at the beginning of the 1950s. It is mitigated by several concessions made to local authorities. Apparently dissatisfaction with the state of things on the part of the leadership of republics and oblasts forced the Soviet rulers to adopt a less strict branch system of economic management. Evidence of this is the resolution on improving regional planning adopted by the CPSU Central Committee and the USSR Council of Ministers in 1979.[15] However, this resolution does not make any sort of substantial change in the existing practice. Investment planning in industry and the regional distribution of investment resources continue to remain with union ministries, which represent branch interests and give the highest priority to satisfying the requirements of projects of all-union significance.

The fact that ministries had investment funds, that branch plans were provided with the necessary material and technical resources, that branches had a huge scientific-research, design, and information base, that all labor resources were transferred branches and most enterprises were subordinate to them—all this transformed branches into powerful economic systems that were not counterbalanced by territorial organs of equal influence in decision making.

The interests of comprehensive regional development plays a subordinate role and often were simply ignored. The nonconvergence of branch and regional interests was an ordinary phenomenon in the practice of planning and designing industry and locating enterprises. The majority of methodological guidelines for determining the effectiveness of investment and most forms of economic analysis were

[15]V. Pavlenko, "Novyi etap v sovershenstvovanii territorial'nogo planirovaniia," *Planovoe khoziaistvo*, 1980, no. 8, pp. 7-17.

based on a branch approach. When used uncritically for the analysis of the effectiveness of developing new areas, they distort economic evaluations of the effectiveness of investment programs for their development.

Why does the branch method of planning and the branch organization of industry hinder the improvement of its regional distribution?

All investment activity of industrial branch ministries is governed by the need to increase the volume of output in the shortest possible time in order to fulfill production plans, and they face strict limitations on capital investment and directives from above to channel the largest part of its into the reconstruction of existing enterprises. The basic idea of capital investments is to save the branch from the immediate danger of failure, during the current five-year plan. And the question of long-term planning of the branch is relegated to secondary status. Such a pragmatic approach keeps branch ministries from giving serious and responsible consideration to long-term planning of the development and location of industrial branches and to general guidelines and optimizing calculations that must objectively consider all negative and positive aspects of the construction of new enterprises in Eastern regions.

Ministries strive to carry out their investment programs primarily in large and medium-size cities, reconstructing and expanding enterprises located there. This makes it possible to use the city's labor, scientific resources, and infrastructure to accelerate the creation and putting into operation of new production capacities.

But the main attractive force, which determines the direction of investment in regions that are already developed, is the availability of construction capabilities in these regions. This seemingly secondary factor is in practice very often decisive in the regional location of new facilities and the expansion and reconstruction of old enterprises. The hypertrophy of branch planning and management of the economy has especially negative consequences for the industrial development of Siberia. Given their narrow branch interests and due to the higher capital intensity of production and the need to create an infrastructure in order to attract workers to the East, industrial ministries prefer to allocate investment to and expand capacity in old industrial regions.

Thus, the narrow branch approach in selecting variants for distributing investments, which is strengthened as limits on investment become stricter, hinders the development of manufacturing industry in Siberia and, hence, gives rise to still greater disproportions in its industrial structure.

UNDERINVESTMENT IN HOUSING AND ITS CONSEQUENCES

A serious obstacle to industrial development of the eastern regions lies in the growing labor deficit due to insufficient investment in social infrastructure. According to the logic of things, the share of Siberia and the Far East in capital investment in the nonproductive sphere of the Soviet economy should be higher than in the regions of the European west. However, this is not the case. For example, the share of capital investment in the nonproductive sphere in the Irkutsk oblast in the 1970s was 23 percent, while the corresponding share for the USSR as a whole was 33 percent.[16] Investment in the development of the social infrastructure is lagging considerably behind population growth in the regions undergoing industrial development, and precisely this is the reason for the limited extent to which the population settles permanently in new areas, the growing labor turnover, and the labor shortage, especially of skilled workers. Thus, at the point of highest investment activity in the Eastern part of the USSR—the Nizhnevartovsk oil and gas region (Tyumen oblast)—where the population grew by a factor of 2.5 in one four-year period (1971-74),[17] the population growth rate during 1965-75 was 1.3 times greater than the rate of growth of capital investment in the social infrastructure.[18] As a result, only 30 to 50 percent of those persons who moved into the region settled permanently, and most of those who left did so within the first two years.[19] The results of a sociological study carried out by the Institute of Economics and the Organization of Industrial Production in newly developing industrial regions of West Siberia showed that the main reason for the outflow of population was the housing shortage.[20] Thus, the amount of new housing provided is the main indicator of the development of the social infrastructure. It would be natural to assume that the share of the Asiatic macrozone in the amount of new housing completed in the country, and especially the share of its northeastern regions, is increasing. However, ananalysis of available statistics does not support this presumption. In 1971-75, as compared with 1966-70, the share of the Asiatic regions in new housing completed remained stable (24.7 and 24.6 percent, respectively),[21] while the share of Siberia

---

[16] *Problemy regional'noi ekonomiki Vostochnoi Sibiri.* Novosibirsk, 1976, p. 46.

[17] V. M. Pushkarev, "Nekotorye problemy formirovaniia Nishnevartovskogo promyshlennogo uzla," *Izvestiia Sibirskogo otdeleniia AN SSSR*, seriia obshchestvennykh nauk, no. 1, vypusk 1, 1976, p. 57.

[18] Ibid., p. 60.

[19] Ibid., p. 61.

[20] *Ekonomicheskie problemy razvitiia Sibiri.* Novosibirsk: Nauka, 1974, pp. 120-121.

[21] *Narkhoz SSSR 1968*, p. 576. *Narkhoz SSSR 1979*, p. 541. *Narkhoz SSSR 1975*, p. 572. *Narkhoz RSFSR 1975*, pp. 340, 351. *Narkhoz UkSSR 1970*, p. 398. *Narkhoz UkSSR 1975*, p. 379.

and the Far East increased by 0.7 percentage points. And here it should be considered that the amount of new housing completed in the USSR as a whole stabilized, and even declined during 1975-78.

In order to determine quantitatively the role assigned to the construction of housing in the eastern regions in Soviet investment policy, we calculated the ratio of the amount of housing completed (in square meters) to the value of fixed capital installed (in millions of rubles) for the USSR as a whole and major regional subdivisions. The values of this ratio for the period 1966-75 are given in Table 8. Judging from the data in this table, housing construction is assuming a smaller and smaller role in Soviet investment activity. But it is more important to note that this decline is much more substantial in regions of the eastern regions than in the European zone.

TABLE 8

RATIOS OF NEW HOUSING CONSTRUCTION TO THE VALUE OF FIXED CAPITAL INSTALLED FOR THE USSR AND MAJOR ZONES[22]

Year	Zone I	Zone II	Zone III
1966-70	1.72	2.14	1.20
1971-75	1.28	1.32	0.88
1970	1.46	1.58	1.05
1971	1.42	1.52	0.95
1972	1.38	1.43	0.97
1973	1.30	1.32	0.87
1974	1.22	1.26	0.86
1975	1.13	1.15	0.78

In light of the facts outlined above, this phenomenon does not seem paradoxical. But it is in sharp contradiction to the logic of the economic development of the eastern regions. It becomes quite clear that the overriding direction of investment is toward productive construction to carry out the narrowly assigned tasks of the present day: to achieve an increase in production in the shortest possible time and by

---

[22]Housing in square meters, fixed capital installed in constant prices, millions of rubles. Zone I includes a group of the most industrially developed regions of the European USSR (Northwest, Central, Volga, Don-Pridnepr, and Ural), Zone II is Kazakhstan and Central Asia, and Zone III is Siberia and the Far East. Sources: See notes to Table 6 and reference 172.

any means.

However, ignoring the necessity of increasing the investment quota of social infrastructure leads to the opposite results. By further and further postponing investment in social infrastructure and permitting an ever greater gap between the increasingly strained investment efforts to expand production capacity and investment in social infrastructure, especially housing, the leadership of the Soviet economy increases the imbalance between the requirements for labor resources and their availability in the eastern regions. The flow of population out of these regions grows, while a positive balance of migration is a decisive condition for fulfilling production programs there.

The lag in the development of social infrastructure as a whole, and especially the lag in housing construction, has in the course of events become one of the main reasons for the reduced rates of growth of oil and gas production in West Siberia. The fact that a conference on stimulating construction in the oil and gas regions of West Siberia was held in the CPSU Central Committee in April 1980 under the direction of Central Committee Secretary for Industry, V. I. Dolgikh,[23] is evidence of growing concern by the Soviet leadership about this matter. One of the central questions of the agenda was a discussion of "the serious shortcomings in the construction of housing." The unusual nature of this conference is reflected in the fact that the participants included not only leaders of construction ministers, Gosplan, and the responsible members of the Party staff, but the directors of major construction organizations that carry out housing construction in Moscow, Leningrad, and the capitals of union republics. It follows from the resolutions of the conference that precisely these organizations must undertake the construction of housing in Siberia. Such measures are taken by the Soviet leadership only in extraordinary cases. Thus, after the earthquake in Tashkent the reconstruction of the wrecked city was assigned to construction organizations from Moscow, Leningrad, and other major cities. The very fact that such a conference was held in 1980 and the sense of the resolutions adopted there suggests the following:

—First, in carrying out the construction program for the Ob'-Irtish territorial-industrial complex, a very difficult situation was created that threatened the fulfillment of plans for the extraction of oil and gas.

—Secondly, the key question in view of the exacerbation of the labor shortage is the accelerated construction of housing and other parts of the social infrastructure.

—Thirdly, the construction industry in Siberia is in no condition to

[23] *Pravda*, April 15, 1980.

handle the volume of work that is needed. This latter fact is a consequence of a long-term tendency to concentrate investment resources overwhelmingly in the development of the construction sector in western regions of the European USSR to the detriment of the eastern regions of the USSR.

THE ROLE OF SIBERIA IN SOVIET INDUSTRY

Judging from official Soviet data, there was only a slow growth in the share of Siberia in the Soviet economy in the post-Khrushchev period (see Table 9).

TABLE 9*

CHANGES IN SIBERIA'S SHARE IN THE ECONOMY OF THE USSR (%)[24]

	1965	1970	1975	1980 (estimate)
Gross social product	8.1	8.5	9.1	9.5
Produced national income	7.5	9.1	10.0	10.5
Gross industrial output	8.1	8.4	9.0	9.2
Capital investment	10.0	11.0	12.0	15.0
Industrial fixed capital	10.5	11.0	13.2	12-13
Construction-assembly work	12.2	12.2	13.2	14-15
Freight hauled, all types of transportation	13.7	14.2	15.7	17-18

*It is possible that the data presented understate Siberia's contribution to gross social product and national income. This understatement arises, first, because the internal wholesale prices on the output of extractive branches are low and the relative prices of the products of several manufacturing branches are high. Second, data on export shipments understate the real role of the region in Soviet exports. Foreign currency earnings from exports of oil and oil products, gas, coal, wood products, and nonferrous metals account for about 50% of the total volume of Soviet exports. The resources which make such exports possible are to a significant extent contributed by Siberia. But the largest part of export shipments reflected in export statistics, are made directly from regions that are closer to foreign-grade ports (for example, oil and gas is shipped from the European part of the USSR).

[24]T. Baranova, "Osnovnye pokazateli razvitiia promyshlennosti Sibiri v desiatoi pyatiletke," *Izvestiia Sibirskogo otdeleniya AN SSSR, seriia obshchestvennych nauk*, no. 11, vypusk 3, 1982, p. 73, *Sibir' v edinom narodnokhozyaztvennom komplekse*, Novosibirsk, Nauka, 1980, p. 19.

In the period since 1965, industrial production in Siberia as a whole has developed at rates somewhat exceeding the national average. But these slightly higher rates are explained by the accelerated production of oil, gas and nonferrous metals, while in the USSR as a whole industrial growth rates have been affected to a greater extent by the forced development of machine-building and the chemical industry.

TABLE 10

GROWTH OF GROSS INDUSTRIAL OUTPUT IN SIBERIA BY BRANCH, 1961-75 (%)[25]

	Average annual rates of growth		
	1961-65	1966-70	1971-75
Power	16.9	12.2	7.6
Fuel (oil, gas, coal)	6.5	9.2	11.3
Ferrous metallurgy	6.9	7.2	4.6
Chemical and petrochemical	22.8	7.4	10.9
Machine-building and metal working	10.2	13.2	9.8
Wood products	5.7	5.8	5.6
Construction materials	9.5	8.7	6.3
Light industry	2.3	12.1	7.6
Food	6.0	5.3	4.6

The contemporary level of industrial production in Siberia is still far from that which was contemplated in substantiating forecasts of economic growth in the USSR based on the natural resource endowment of that half of the country. The share of Siberia in Soviet industrial production at present does not exceed 10 percent, and for machine-building, chemicals, construction materials, light and food industry, it is substantially lower.

Thus, a high rate of growth of production is characteristic of a relatively narrow group of branches in Siberian industry. These are almost exclusively branches in the initial stages of the production cycle, involved primarily in supplying consumers outside Siberia and only

[25] *Narkhoz SSSR v 1965*, pp. 126, 129. *Narkhoz SSSR v 1975*, pp. 190-91, 196-97, 204-09, 212-14, 221-22. *Narkhoz RSFSR v 1975*, pp. 88-89, 91, 93-96, 100-03, 110-13, 121, 124, 128, 132-36.

weakly participating in the formation of a balanced and integrated economy in Siberia itself. The development of Siberian industry is characterized above all by the forced development of the extractive branches and the extraordinarily slow expansion of the manufacturing industry. During the past two decades there has been a tendency for this disproportion to increase. The share of extractive industry in Siberia is 2.3 times higher than the average for the USSR.[26] The share of manufacturing industry is correspondingly lower. Branches of industry that produce final products (machine-building and light and food industry) have significantly lower shares in Siberia than in the USSR as a whole: 47 percent and 63 percent respectively.[27]

Industry in Siberia is developing primarily as a national supplier of fuel, raw materials, nonferrous metals, and timber. Such a direction in the region contradicts the thesis of priority (and balanced, harmonious) development of the eastern regions of the country that has been declared during the entire history of Soviet power. In fact, throughout this period and especially in recent decades Siberia has developed as a narrowly oriented part of the national economic system—as a region with an economy specialized in a few products.

The industrial development of Siberia is lagging considerably behind the planned rate (see Table 11).

TABLE 11

PLANNED AND ACTUAL GROWTH OF GROSS INDUSTRIAL OUTPUT (%)[28]

	1959-65 plan act.	1966-70 plan act.	1971-75 plan act.	1976-80 plan act.
USSR	180 184	150 150	147 143	135 124
Siberia	250 185	166 154	163 151	150 130

[26]T. Baranova, "Osnovnye pokazateli razvitiia promyshlennosti Sibiri v sed'moi deviatoi piatiletkakh," *Izvestiia Sibirskogo otdeleniia AN SSSR, seriia obshchestvennykh nauk*, no. 1, vypusk 1, 1979, p. 30.
[27]Sibir' v edinom ..., p. 36.
[28]*KPSS v rezoliutsiiakh i pesheniiakh s"ezdov*, no. 12, Moscow, Izdatel'stvo politicheskoi literatury, 1978, pp. 192-93. *Pravda*, 28 February 1981, report by N. Tikhonov. A. Granberg, "Narodnokhoziaistvenaia effektivnost' uskorennogo razvitiia proizvoditel'nykh sil Sibiri," *Planovoe khoziaistvo*, no. 5, 1981, p. 74. *Tendentsii ekonomicheskogo razvitiia Sibiri*, Novosibirsk, Nauka, 1980, p. 52.

It is taking place under the stamp of a policy of devoting all efforts to the forced development of the fuel-energy complex. But this is being achieved at the expense of an increasing lag in manufacturing industry and the infrastructure. Investment activity in Siberia is aggravating the disproportions in the industrial structure and slowing the development of production that the region actually needs.

INVESTMENT IN SIBERIAN INDUSTRY AND DEVELOPMENT OF OIL AND GAS PRODUCTION

Industrial development in Siberia has been restrained primarily by insufficient investment in manufacturing industry. Between 1965 and 1975 the the share of Siberia and the Far East in investment in the economy of the USSR as a whole increased by less than one percentage point. More recently the share of the fuel industry has been growing at an accelerated pace, but the rate of growth of investment in the region's other sectors has fallen.[29] Thus, the underinvestment in Siberia's manufacturing industry has become even worse.

Even the petrochemical industry has been starved for investment funds and, as a result, its development in Siberia absolutely does not correspond to the rapid growth of oil production. Only about 7 percent of the country's investment in the petrochemical industry in 1971-75 was in Siberia.[30] At the same time, the overwhelming part of new production capacities for chemical fibers, synthetic rubber and synthetic resins and plastics have been located in the European regions of the country, which are experiencing a shortage of fuel and water. The insufficiency of investment has led to the fact that, in spite of the resource saving possibilities of the region, the rates of growth of chemical and petrochemical output have slowed and been below the national rates. The growth of mineral fertilizers, synthetic resins and plastics, and synthetic fibers has declined sharply. The construction of new enterprises was curtailed and construction was slowed on oil-gas-chemical complexes started at Tomsk, Tobol'sk, Omsk, and elsewhere.

The branch structure of industrial capital investment in Siberia in general reflects the structure of production and differs noticeably from the national structure. While the largest share of investment in industry in the USSR as a whole goes to machine-building, in Siberia this branch gets a relatively small share.

---

[29] *Narkhoz SSSR v 1965*, p. 528. *Narkhoz SSSR v 1975*, p. 502. *Narkhoz RSFSR v 1975*, p. 374. *Narkhoz RSFSR v 1975*, p. 502. T. Baranova, "Dinamika zaniatosti, proizvoditel'nosti truda i osnovnykh proizvodsvennykh fondov v promyshlennost' Sibiri," *Izvestiia Sibirskogo otdeleniia AN SSSR, seriia ekonomicheskaya.*

[30] *Sibir' v edinom narodnokhoziaistvennom komplekse*, p. 24.

From one five-year plan to the next, the share of the electric power branch in total Soviet industrial investment grows. Siberia is characterized by the opposite trend. The share of investment in ferrous metallurgy in Siberia is lower than in the country as a whole. Its trends also do not coincide with the national tendency: the share of ferrous metallurgy in industrial capital investment for the USSR declined in 1966-70 and increased in 1971-75. In Siberia it has been declining for a long time. An analogous picture is observed in investment in chemicals and petrochemicals. The investment shares of the food and construction materials industries in Siberia are also declining.[31] In speaking of the insufficiency of investment in Siberia's manufacturing industry, it is necessary to keep in mind that in Siberia, to a greater extent than in other regions, the investment process is of an extensive nature. This characteristic is manifested as follows:

First, in Siberia relatively larger capital investments are required per unit of output, and a certain part of this additional capital intensiveness is due to objective factors (natural and climatic conditions and the underdevelopment of the infrastructure).

Second, the share of investment in the renovation and modernization of existing production facilities here is much lower than the average for the USSR or, even more so, the European part of the country.

Third, the share of unfinished construction is much higher in Siberia. In 1975 it amounted to 86 percent of annual capital investment in West Siberia and 124 percent in East Siberia, while the average for the USSR was 75 percent.[32] This higher share of unfinished construction is explained in part by the shortcomings of Siberia's construction industry.

As investment activity has shifted to the north, the significance of extensive factors has increased. Thus, due to the more difficult natural climatic and economic-geographic conditions, the investment required per unit of output in the gas industry is 70 percent greater in the higher latitudes than in middle latitudes.[33] Obviously, an ever growing share of investment will be devoured by the increasing expensiveness of construction and correspondingly less will be left for net increases in production.

---

[31] *Narkhoz SSSR v 1965*, p. 528. *Narkhoz SSSR v 1975*, p. 502. *Narkhoz RSFSR v 1965*, p. 374. *Narkhoz RSFSR v 1975*, p. 502. T. Baranova, "Dinamika zaniatosti, proizvoditel'nosti truda i osnovnykh prizvodennykh fondov v promyshlennosti Sibiri," *Izvestiia Sibirskogo otdeleniia AN SSSR, seriia obshchestvennykh nauk*, no. 6, vypusk 2, 1980, p. 110.

[32] *Sibir' v edinom narodnokhoziaistvennom komplekse*, p. 13.

[33] I. Kariagin, V. Bulatov, and V. Tandalov, *Razvitie gazovoi promyshlennosti severa Tyumenskoi oblasti*, Moscow, Nedra, 1979, p. 31.

Judging from the plan for 1981-85, the increasing emphasis on investment in the fuel branches at the expense of other industrial branches will continue in the current decade. These trends will be manifested especially sharply in the investment structure of industry in Siberia, which is to supply practically the entire increase in production of oil, gas, and coal for the USSR.

TABLE 12

GROWTH OF FUEL PRODUCTION IN SIBERIA, STANDARD FUEL UNITS[34]

	1965-70	1970-75	1975-80
Gas	11.1	31.4	159.3
Oil	44.4	170.2	240.9
Coal	14.5	25.7	13.9

TABLE 13

SHARES OF GAS, OIL, AND COAL IN SIBERIAN FUEL PRODUCTION, STANDARD FUEL UNITS (%)

	1965	1970	1975	1980
Gas	0.01	6.6	10.8	25.2
Oil	1.41	26.6	54.0	55.8
Coal	98.58	66.8	35.2	19.0

The task set for the current decade is to "offset oil with gas." The essence of the energy policy planned for the 1980s is to substitute gas and coal for liquid fuel in electric power stations and boilers in order to maximize the satisfaction of oil needs for nonfuel needs and export. It has become popular among Soviet energy specialists to quote Dmitri Mendeleev: "Oil is not heating fuel. You can burn bank notes to stay warm."

[34] Iu. Maksimov, "Dobycha toplivno-energeticheskikh resursov v Sibiri," *Izvestiia Sibirskogo otdeleniia AN SSSR, seriia obshchestvennykh nauk*, no. 6, vypusk 2, 1982, p. 34.

In 1981-83 the production of gas is planned to grow by 50 percent, which is five times greater than the growth of oil extraction (with gas condensate). In 1981-85, the entire increment of gas extraction is slated to be provided by production from the Urengoi field in West Siberia.[35] In 1980 the correlation of oil and gas (in standard fuel units) in total production of the West Siberian oil-gas complex was 7:3. In 1985 this correlation is planned to change to 55:45, and in the second half of the 1980s the share of gas, according to the plan, should exceed that of oil.[36] Thus, the West Siberian "oil-gas" complex is going to turn into the "gas-oil" complex. Another feature of this period is the development of the Kansk-Achinsk coal basin and, in connection with this, the expected stabilization and then increase in the share of coal in Siberian fuel production.

In 1965-70 the Siberian fuel industry provided less than one-fourth of the increment in the country's extraction of basic fuel resources; in 1970-75 its share was more than two-thirds. In 1975-80 the Siberian fuel industry not only provided the entire increase in production but compensated for a decline in production in several oil and coal producing regions of the country. According to the plan for 1981-85, more than half of the country's basic fuel resources will be produced in Siberia, and the entire investment policy for Siberia is aimed at achieving this goal.

Thus, investment trends will even further increase the disproportion between extractive and manufacturing industry in Siberia.

---

[35]I. Nikonenko and B. Orlov, "Voprosy sozdaniia novoi gazodobyvaiushei bazy," *Izvestiia Sibirskogo otdeleniia AN SSSR, seriia obshchestvennykh nauk*, no. 11, vypusk 3, 1981, pp. 123, 124.
[36]Yu. Maksimov, "Dobycha toplivno-energeticheskikh resursov v Sibiri," p. 36.

CHAPTER FIVE

THE CONCEPT OF SIBERIAN INDUSTRIAL DEVELOPMENT AND ITS IMPLEMENTATION

Logical analysis allows us to outline [various] possible alternatives for the economical development of Siberia in the '80s. These can be viewed to a certain extent as scenarios of the future.

SCENARIO NO. 1: The further concentration of efforts to develop all-nation energy-fuel and raw-material bases in Siberia, primarily orienting their output to delivery to the European part (including the Ural region), with a relatively small growth of manufacturing industries in Siberia. This is the least efficient way to develop Siberia's production potential—it leads to a disproportionate increase in transport expenditures and prevents the complex utilization of primary and intermediary output of the production sphere of the economy .... .

Bearing in mind the great inertia of the existing territorial proportions in the national economy, the growing strain on the balances of capital investments and labor resources throughout the country as a whole, and the primary orientation toward modernization and renovation of existing plants and factories, we can expect that at first the development of Siberia's production potential will gravitate more toward the first scenario....

Prof. Boris Orlov, leading expert on Siberian development, 1982

If we formulate in condensed form the conception of accelerated industrial development in Siberia on a long-term basis as it was elaborate in the 1960s by scientific and design organizations which undertook econometric studies based on an optimizing interregional input-output model, its basic ideas would reduce to the following:

- Maintain high rates of growth of the output of extractive branches, especially fuels.

- At the same time, force the development of manufacturing industry, especially machine-building. The growth rates of machine-building production in West Siberia should substantially exceed the growth of fuel output.

- Locate energy-intensive production in the region on a priority basis, since huge fuel and energy resources are concentrated in the region and the technical and economic parameters for their extraction greatly exceed the corresponding indicators in other regions of the country.

- The level of electricity use in the economy should be especially high, much higher than for the USSR as a whole (a correlation of 3:2) since in addition to the fact that it is expedient to concentrate production with electricity-intensive technology in Siberia, the region is distinguished by its extreme constraints on labor resources. Therefore, the use of electric power for the automation of production processes and as a substitute for manual labor in all spheres of the economy should be as great as possible in Siberia.

- Thus, a leading role in the industrial development of Siberia should be played by electric power. The production of power should exceed the production of fuel and, in general, surpass the growth of industrial production in the region.

How is this conception working out in practice? At the very same time that the oil and gas industry of Siberia is rapidly developing, growth in the production of electrical energy and in machine-building production has substantially decreased. Compared to the average annual growth rates for 1966-70, in 1976-80 the growth tempo for both of these two industries had fallen approximately twofold. Siberia's share of the all-union production of electrical energy and machine-building has decreased, while its share in the production of fuel has sharply increased.

Now we may rightfully conclude that this conception, with the exception of the first point, was in no way realized. Moreover, the trend toward transforming Siberia into a fuel-energy appendage for the industrial development of the western regions of the country is increasing.

Thus electrical energy and machine-building—which were intended to play the main role in the development of an advanced industry in Siberia—have in fact not done so. The result is a highly paradoxical phenomenon.

TABLE 14

SIBERIA'S SHARE IN USSR GROSS OUTPUT BY BRANCH, %[1]

	1960	1965	1970	1975	1980
Fuel	12.8	14.6	17.0	21.1	26.7
Electrical Energy	11.3	13.6	5.5	15.3	15.0
Machine-building	9.7	7.5	8.1	7.7	7.4

TABLE 15

SIBERIA'S SHARE IN THE INCREMENTS TO GROSS OUTPUT FOR THE USSR BY BRANCH, %[2]

	1961-65	1966-70	1971-75	1976-80
Fuel	23.6	24.1	38.4	59.3
Electrical Energy	16.1	19.0	18.0	13.9
Machine-building	5.6	8.8	6.7	6.6

THE PARADOX OF ELECTRICAL ENERGY

Thus, the very foundations of Siberian economic development was the creation of an enormous surfeit of electrical-energy capacity. And no resources were begrudged for a quarter of a century in an effort to attain this goal. But lo and behold: Siberia now suffers an acute shortage of electrical energy, which is obstructing the development of manufacturing industries and thereby the entire economy of the region.

The foundation of electrical power in Siberia is its Unified Power System, which supplies about 90 percent of consumers in the region and has a unique structure: almost half of the overall capacity of its component electric stations comes from highly economical hydroelectric stations, the largest of which is the Krasnoiarsk.[3] While the distribution of overall capacity between thermoelectric and hydroelectric

---

[1]T. Baranova, "Osnovnye pokazateli razvitiia promyshlennosti Sibiri v desyatoi pyatiletke," p. 73. *Sibir' v edinom narodnokhoziaistvennom komplekse*, Novosibirsk, Nauka, 1980, pp. 33, 34.

[2]Loc cit.

[3]*Sibir' v edinom narodnokhoziaistvennom komplekse*, p. 143.

plants in the power system in the European part of the country is 86:14, in the Siberian power system this correlation is 52:48.[4] This structure in combination with cheap fuel has given the Siberian Unified Power System the lowest expenditures on electricity in the country: Siberian power is 40-60 percent cheaper than in the European regions of the country.

The intensive development of hydroelectric power, which was to play a leading role in the development of Siberia's industrial complex, was the object of an extensive investment program in the 1950s and 1960s located primarily in Krasnoiarsk krai and Irkutsk oblast'.

During 1965-80 the production of power in Siberia increased 2.6-fold. However, the rate of development of power in Siberia has steadily declined the average annual rate of growth fell from 16 percent in 1961-65 to 4 percent in 1976-80.[5] Here it is important to distinguish the following two trends: first, the growth of power production in Siberia has lagged behind national growth rates, and, second, in the 1970s there was a tendency for the growth of power production to fall behind the growth of total industrial production in Siberia.

How can it be that a region that in all economic forecasts and all long-term plans of the Soviet economy was always viewed as a region with surplus electric power (a surplus arising from huge investments over the course of decades) could suddenly turn into a region with a power shortage?

1. THE POWER SHORTAGE IN SIBERIA AND ITS CAUSES

The power shortage that appeared in the 1970s and is tending to become more serious is the direct result of a distortion in investment in Siberian power the predominance of investment in hydroelectric power and the extremely limited investment in thermoelectric power. Such a policy, implemented throughout the 1950s and 1960s, turned out to be a major miscalculation by Soviet planners and designers. The consequences of this error will weigh heavily on the economic development of Siberia in the remaining two decades of this century. In addition to this, the construction of massive hydroelectric stations led to the flooding of vast areas of agricultural land, forests, and as yet undeveloped sites of mineral raw materials and has also had a significant impact on the region's climate (in particular, Krasnoiarsk). In short, the ecological consequences are no less severe and will last incomparably longer than the economic.

---

[4] *Energetika SSSR v 1976-1980 gg.*, Moscow, Energiia, 1977, p. 165.
[5] *Narkhoz 1980*, p. 154. T Baranova, "Osnovnye pokazateli," 1979, p. 31, 1982, p. 74.

In the 1970's an incompatibility developed between the structure of generating capacities and Siberia's power requirements. Generating capacities increased primarily as a result of hydroelectric stations and almost no new thermal powerplant capacities were put into operation. As a result a situation developed in which surplus capacities were formed at hydroelectric stations that maintained a low load level throughout the year, while there was a shortfall in thermal powerplant capacities that might have offset seasonal declines in production hydroelectric plants.

In building the Krasnoiarsk hydroelectric station (with an annual capacity of six billion kilowatt-hours, the largest not only in the USSR but in the world), which was to provide practically the increase in Siberian power production in the 1970's, an inconsistency was permitted between parameters of the reservoir intended for the annual and seasonal regulation of water flow and turbine capacity. The station's power generating equipment could not provide an even output on both an annual and seasonal basis and still maintain a water throughout sufficient for intensive ship traffic on the Yenisei—an important meridianal transportation artery in Siberia. Therefore, the station works at half capacity throughout the year. The low utilization of this giant of electric power led to the development of a very serious situation with power in Angaro-Yenisei region (Krasnoiarsk krai and Irkutsk oblast') where it is located. And this is one of the most important industrial regions in Siberia.

The excessive increase in the construction of powerful hydroelectric stations in East Siberia led to the development of surplus hydroelectric capacities and a catastrophic shortfall in capacities at thermal powerplants where production does not depend on natural conditions. It turned out that reserve capacities should have been precisely in the thermal powerplants for which investment funds for construction and expansion were not allocated.

To get a complete impression of the existing situation, the particulars of power consumption in Siberia must be considered. It is characterized by highly concentrated use both on a daily and an annual basis the average annual duration of maximum load is about 7,000 hours. At the same time. for many years the number of hours of utilization of the Krasnoiarsk hy hydroelectric station has been about 3,500 hours.[6] Thermal powerplants must compensate for the shortfall in output of hydroelectric stations during periods of low water flow. However, due to capacity limitations they are unable to do this.

---

[6] *Sibir' v edinom narodnokhoziaistvennom komplekse*, p. 144.

One other significant factor must be added to this: the lag in the development of the electrical network of Siberia's Unified Power System. The vastness of the territory served, the high concentration of capacities, and the relatively weakly developed electrical network noticeably reduces the quality and reliability of the electric supply to several regions of central Siberia.

Thus, Siberia became a power-short region and wasted the advantage a region with significant energy capacity reserves that made it attractive for the development of energy-intensive production in spite of relative capital costs that were higher in comparison with other regions of the country. The difficulties with the power supply continue to grow. Strict limitations on the consumption of power have been instituted throughout Siberia, including for energy-intensive production.

The strained situation with electric power became an additional factor hindering ministries from locating manufacturing industry enterprises in Siberia.

At the present time the only thing that might ease the situation is an increase in the utilization of thermal powerplant capacities in critical periods. To what extent can this possibility be realized?

The problem of utilizing thermal powerplant capacities in Siberia is apparently more acute than in many other regions of the USSR. One of the basic conditions of a reliable power supply is the availability of a certain reserve generating capacity. It is generally considered in the USSR that the power system should have the following reserves: for accidents, in case a generating unit goes out of operation (about 3-5%), which is a minimally necessary condition for reliability of the power supply; peak load, in case of increases in consumers' requirements (2-3%); repair (5-6%); and economic (3-5%) as a precondition for creating new or expanding existing capacities. All together, in the opinion of specialists, power system reserves should be a minimum of 10-12%, and 13-15% is desirable.

In fact, in the mid-1970's the Siberian Unified Power System had only insignificant reserves for equipment repair—much less than the norms require. The power shortage gives rise to an excessively high load on thermal powerplants above all norms. In 1975, for example, the average number of hours of operation for the thermal powerplants in the USSR as a whole was 5,741, while the average for the Siberian Unified Power System was 6,600 hours.[7] For several powerplants this figure was 7,200-7,500 hours. Such forced loading excludes the possibility for timely repair of equipment which causes it to wear out more

---

[7] *Narkhoz SSSR v 1975*, p. 237. *Ocherki ekonomiki Sibiri*, Novosibirsk, Nauka, 1980, p. 1969.

rapidly. The possibilities for replacing old equipment with new are being reduced from year to year because of the decline in its production in the USSR. The production of turbines has stabilized at the level of the late 1970's, and the production of turbine generators and steam boilers has declined. Even more significant is the fact that the amount of new capacity for the production of turbines introduced in 1976-80 declined in comparison with 1971-75 by almost 50% on an average annual basis.[8]

Given such an overloading of the operation of thermal powerplants, the absence of reserve capacities in the Unified Power System, and the difficult situation with power in the region, it is absolutely impossible to take some powerplant out of operation for a time for the reconstruction and modernization of equipment.

It follows that the output of power in Siberia can be increased only by greater utilization of the capacities of hydroelectric stations. And the paradox of the existing situation is, thus, that climatic conditions play just as important a role in the power production and power supply of Siberia as in the region's agriculture.

Eliminating the shortage of power in Siberia will be a long process. It will require a fundamental restructuring of the Unified Power System in the direction of increasing the share of production of power at thermal powerplants. The optimal distribution of production of power between thermal and hydroelectric stations in Siberia must be a ratio of 75:25 in the opinion of Soviet specialists[9] (remember that now it is 52:48). The tasks involved is to convert thermal powerplants from liquid to hard fuel, i.e., coal. The plan for solving this sizable problem is to create and develop a system of thermal powerplants using cheap coal from the Kansk-Achinsk basin.

2. THE KANSK-ACHINSK NODE

Without exaggeration we may say that the development of electric power in Siberia in the 1980's will depend primarily on the pace and scale of exploitation of the coal fields in the Kansk-Achinsk basin. But the development of these deposits and bringing their coal into the country's fuel-energy balance goes far beyond regional problems in Siberia; it is one of the most important tasks for the Soviet economy in the current decade.

The solution of the Kansk-Achinsk problem, like any other economic problem of this scale, is permeated with sharp contradictions which it has taken decades to overcome. These contradictions, which

[8] *Narkhoz SSSR 1980*, pp. 165, 329.
[9] *Sibir' v edinom narodnokhoziaistvennom komplekse*, p. 146.

are of an entirely objective nature, to this day give rise to bitter arguments that by themselves, naturally, create considerable difficulties in the planning and design processes, whether it is Gosplan, the Academy of Sciences, a ministry or design institute. The Kansk-Achinsk basin adjoins the Kuznets coal basin, and these two basins in the southern part of central Siberia account for almost 68% of the country's coal reserves that are favorable for economic development.

Given Siberian conditions the location of the Kansk-Achinsk basin is exceptionally favorable. Its good mining and geological conditions are supplemented by the existence in that zone of southern Siberia of large and medium-size cities, developed agriculture, and a convenient location with respect to transportation ties: the basic deposits are located in direct proximity to existing railroad lines and others that are under construction. The entire length of the basin is crossed by the Trans-Siberian Railroad, from which the Achinsk-Abakan line runs to the south and the Achinsk-Yenisei line to the north. Apparently in the not too distant future the basin will also receive a link to the Middle-Siberian Mainline. An exceptionally important factor is the location of the basin, especially its southern part, adjacent to main centers of Siberian industry—Novosibirsk, Kemerovo, Krasnoiarsk, Novokuznetsk, and Tomsk. The basic concentrations of metallurgy, petrochemicals and chemicals, machine-building and construction materials are located precisely in these regions of southern Siberia. At the same time, these are regions with the most developed, by Siberian standards, infrastructure. Thus, these are the most fuel-short regions.

The Conception of Utilizing Kansk-Achinsk and Kuznets Basin Coal

The main question that gives rise to contradictory opinions is the division of functions between the Kansk-Achinsk and Kuznets basins.

Kansk-Achinsk coal is now and will in the future be the cheapest fuel in the country. Its coal is 2-2.5 times cheaper to extract than Kuznets coal (in standard fuel units) and 7-8 times cheaper than Donets coal.[10] Therefore, it is in the interests of the economy of the USSR to expand the mining and consumption of Kansk-Achinsk coal as much as possible and thus to release oil and gas for qualified users (not fuel uses), exports, and other needs, and to supply Kuznets coal to fuel-short regions of the Urals and the European part of the USSR.

The hypothesis about the development and use of the coal resources of southern Siberia that existed until recently was based on two fundamental postulates: 1) The Kuznets basin was viewed as the

[10]Ibid., p. 147.

basic supplier of coking coal for metallurgy in the Urals and Siberia. At the same time not much significance was attributed to the development of the energy coal of this basin. 2) The energy coal of the Kansk-Achinsk basin should be used to cover the power shortage in the Urals and the European part of the USSR. And only about half of its coal was intended for use in Siberia itself—primarily for the needs of the central part of Krasnoiarsk krai.

The Irkutsk and Minusinsk basins and deposits in Zabaikal, were supposed to supply East Siberia with coal.

However, in the mid-1970's new factors arose—new factors in the energy situation both for the country as a whole and for Siberia, which led to the formation of new ideas about the development of the Kansk-Achinsk basin.

First, there was an orientation toward eliminating the power shortage in the European regions primarily by constructing atomic power plants (already in 1976-80, 35% of the increase in capacity of electric power stations in the European regions was to be provided by atomic power).[11]

Second, a reevaluation of the possibilities of the Kuznets basin showed that the maximum level of extraction might be increased almost two fold. At the same time, the prospects for extracting transportable fuel coal increased substantially, and new possibilities for reducing the cost of production arose.

According to contemporary estimates the potential for extracting coal in Kuznets basin is put at a minimum of 550 million tons per year, including approximately 200 million tons of coking coal and 350 million tons of fuel coal.[12] At present about 40 million tons of Kuznets coal are consumed in Siberia itself. Experts believe that even if consumption in Siberia increases to 50-60 million tons the Kuznets basin could still ship 280-300 million tons of coal to the European part of the country and the Urals (250-270 million tons of standard fuel).[13] For comparison we will note that coal extraction in the Donetsk basin amounts to about 150 million tons. Thus, in addition to supplying coking coal the Kuznets basin could become an important supplier of fuel for power in European regions of the country. A decline in the growth of iron smelting by the classical blast-furnace method in the USSR and also a decline in the relative amount of coke used in iron smelting will lead to a reduction in requirements for coking coal, the production of which still continues to be viewed as the main task of the Kuznets basin.

[11] *Energetika SSSR v 1976-1980 gg.*, p. 114.
[12] *Ocherki ekonomiki Sibiri*, p. 129.
[13] *Sibir' v edinom narodnokhoziaistvennom komplekse*, p. 146.

These circumstances plus the closer location of the region to regions of consumption (the Kuznets region is located about 300 kilometers west of the Kansk-Achinsk) will substantially increase the role of Kuznets coal in the fuel balance of the Urals and the European regions of the country.

The economic effectiveness of using Kansk-Achinsk coal is higher the closer the consumer is to the point of extraction. More than 140 billion tons of the coal reserves are estimated to be suitable for open-pit mining. But the brown coal of the Kansk-Achinsk basin is distinguished by its high moisture content (from 28 to 43%) and as a result has a tendency to oxidize and even ignite spontaneously. Therefore, it is not suitable for long-distance shipment or long-term storage. Unlike Kansk-Achinsk coal, Kuznets basin coal is highly transportable and does not require any sort of preliminary processing.

In the opinion of a former Minister of Power and Electrification who was subsequently director of the Krzhizhanovskii Energy Institute, Dmitri Zhimerin, transporting Kansk-Achinsk coal long distances is extremely undesirable.[14] Transmitting power produced from Kansk-Achinsk coal near where it is mined to the European part of the country by direct current lines would involve huge expenditures on the construction of powerful transmission lines. Thus, this approach to using Kansk-Achinsk coal to feed the energy system of European regions is also rather doubtful.

All these considerations suggest that the most expedient approach both for the near and distant future is to use the coal and power from the Kansk-Achinsk basin entirely for Siberia's needs and to aid the fuel short regions of the European part of the country with oil and gas from West Siberia and Kuznets basin coal. In this case the main user of Kansk-Ahinsk basin energy (70-80%) will be central Siberia, primarily its southern part, which possesses significant resources for the development of energy-intensive production from the standpoint of its construction base, infrastructure, and relatively skilled work force.

Thus, the construction of powerful thermal powerplants on the territory of the basin and in the surrounding area within 200-300 kilometers would turn the Kansk-Achinsk fuel-energy complex into a primary energy base for Siberia, and the low cost of power would make all other regions of the country uncompetitive with the southern part of central Siberia from the standpoint of the economic effectiveness of the development of energy-intensive production. That is the idea.

---

[14]Ibid., p. 148.

But the realization of the idea involves the solution of the following very complex economic, technological, and ecological problems.

Problems of Implementing the Kansk-Achinsk-Kuznets Concept

First: increasing the extraction of fuel coal from the Kuznets basin to 300-350 million tons (the approximate amount to compensate for not shipping Kansk-Achinsk coal to the west) will require the thorough construction and technical retooling of many Kuznets basin mines.

Second: transporting coal from the Kuznets basin to the Urals and European region will require the construction of special roads or pipelines. At the end of the 1970's, 30-40 million tons of coal were being shipped to the Urals and the European part of the USSR from the Kuznets basin. Shipping as much as 250-300 million tons of Kuznets coal (which, incidentally, is the equivalent of another Donets basin appearing in the European part of the USSR) would be a much more difficult task given the catastrophic overloading of main transportation arteries and the accelerating growth in the flow of oil and gas in the same direction.

Third: a high concentration of coal mining and power production at thermal powerplants in the most densely populated region of Siberia would threaten the environment and make it dangerous for human habitation. Judging from the long-range plan, it is anticipated that by the end of the century a group of thermal powerplants with an overall capacity of up to 50 million kwh will be located in the western part of the basin within a distance of 100-200 kilometers of each other. It is proposed that about 200-250 million tons of natural fuel will be burned at these stations. Even with an ash discharge of 5-7%, the total quantity of ash and cinders could be 12-15 million tons a year. Designs to deal with these discharges envision the construction of smokestacks 360 meters high (with a diameter at the most of 14 meters).[15] In this case the area over which particles are spread and settle will increase, but the atmosphere will still be dusty and in the long run a significant area of the densely populated region of Siberia will be polluted. We may add to this the huge consumption of oxygen in burning such a quantity of fuel. And a similar pollution problem will arise with water resources. The single major river here—Chulym—already supplies water to and receives waste from the growing Kansk-Achinsk industrial center, and its potential is near exhaustion. The diversion of water from the Yenisei to the Chulym could be a real escape from this situation, but this, of course, would involve major hydrotechnical construction.

---

[15] *Ocherki ekonomiki Sibiri*, p. 173.

It should be kept in mind that the ecological condition of the territory adjacent to the western flank of the Kansk-Achinsk and Kuznets basins is already generating concern among Soviet ecologists and physicians. The situation has become especially serious in a center of Siberian metallurgy—Novokuznetsk. Among other factors that are damaging the environment and dangerous for man, of particular concern are the consequences of introducing electric-arc steel production technology in the process of reconstructing the giant Kuznets metallurgical combine without the necessary technology to render production waste harmless. Here is what the director of the Siberian Institute of Occupational Health, V. Bessonenko, has to say about this: "For example, we are very disturbed by the expansion of electric-arc steel production *at the same technical level that exists in the branch* [my emphasis, B.R.]. The point is that both in working conditions and in generating wastes of such components as chrome, selenium, and nickel, this technology is much more dangerous an open-hearth production, to say nothing of convertors."[16] And it is precisely electrometallurgy that is slated to be developed using the cheap power in the Kansk-Achinsk fuel-energy complex.

Four: is the pernicious consequences of energy and industrial capacities for the highly intensive agriculture of the region, for the fertile high-yield soil. In addition to discharges into the atmosphere and water pollution, the region's agriculture will inevitably be affected by the removal of huge areas of arable land from agricultural use, which can hardly be offset by increases in the productivity of the remaining land. The latter factor and large population growth resulting from the development of industry will increase the shortage of agricultural products in the region, a deficit that must be covered by additional shipments from other regions of the country. And we should note that it is specifically the regions adjacent to the Kansk-Achinsk basin that are Siberia's granary.

Five: is the creation of a construction complex. A comparison of the requirements for construction work with existing construction capabilities shows that the construction base must almost be created anew. The existing capacity of the construction complex is hardly sufficient for the creation of a pioneering construction base The projected construction of several machine-building enterprises (the Krasnoiarsk heavy excavator plant, electric machine-building plant and others) will divert capacities of the region's construction organizations that are already used to the limit. Judging from the lack of coordination that has characterized the construction of the first projects for future Kansk-

---

[16]*EKO*, no. 2, 1978, p. 108.

Achinsk thermal powerplants (housing and structures for the construction industry), this investment program is being implemented in the worst tradition of Soviet mass-scale construction.

Six: is the decline in the production of equipment for the coal industry and turbines for powerplants, which has become more serious in the early 1980s[17] and which must necessarily affect the supply of equipment to Kansk-Achinsk thermal powerplant projects.

In order to carry out the Kansk-Achinsk thermal powerplant program, fundamentally new technology and huge capital investments and labor resources will be necessary. Given the contemporary economic situation and technical level, the implementation of this program will proceed at a very slow pace, with a number of palliative decisions being taken, and with alternating dampened and flourishing stages in the construction cycle. The only thing that could breathe life into this project and intensify its development is Western credits and an increase in imports. It is impossible to imagane that, given the existing political situation in the country, there are any other possibilities.

Thus, there is no reason to expect any easing of the electric power situation in Siberia in the forseeable future from the development of the Kansk-Achinsk thermal powerplant program. It would appear that the situation will not be significantly corrected until at least the end of this decade.

THE PARADOX OF THE MACHINE-BUILDING INDUSTRY

Notwithstanding the sharply growing demand for machines and equipment, notwithstanding the great difficulties of creating and developing the production of these items in Siberia itself (above all, given its labor shortage), even that extremely inadequate quantity which *is* produced is transferred far beyond its perimeters—to other regions of the USSR. At this very same time, to satisfy Siberia's own needs, machines and equipment are shipped in from the western regions of the USSR—over enormous distances, on a critically overloaded railway system.

1. TRENDS IN SIBERIAN MACHINE-BUILDING AND ITS ROLE IN USSR PRODUCTION

The rate of development of Siberian machine-building does not at all conform to the region's growing requirements. After 1960 machine-building was developed most intensively in the central and western regions of the USSR, and the construction of new machine-

---

[17] *Pravda*, 24 April 1982.

building plants in Siberia was almost stopped. The average annual rate of growth of machine-building output declined from 13.1 percent in 1955-60 to 9.8 percent in 1971-75.[18] And Siberia's share in national machine-building production declined from 9.7 percent in 1960 to 7.4 percent in 1980.[19]

The slowing of the development of machine-building, which is characteristic not only of Siberia but the country as a whole, is explained by several factors common to all Soviet machine-building including such things as the aging of equipment, the shortage and low quality of metal, and the reduction in the average number of shifts worked. But in addition an important role is played by the negative attitude of branch ministries to investment in Siberian machine-building due to the higher relative capital costs there and the problems with the labor supply (the average number of shifts that Siberian machine-building enterprises operate does not exceed 1.4)[20] and the growing power shortage. The absence of any desire to expand the capacity of Siberian machine-building is apparent in the fact that in the first half of the 1970s, for example, the region's capital investment in machine-building amounted to only about 4-5 percent of total investment in machine-building in the USSR.[21]

The recent lag of Siberian machine-building behind the region's requirements stands out in comparing the trends of growth in industry and machine-building output against the background of analogous processes in the Soviet economy as a whole (see table 16). While the growth trends of machine-building and industrial output in Siberia roughly paralleled those for the USSR as a whole in the 1960s, in 1971-75 the extent to which machine-building growth exceeded overall industrial growth increased for the USSR but dropped for Siberia. The development of Siberian machine-building has also lagged behind the overall development of the machine-building industry in the USSR. This is evident from the data for 1961-75 in table 17 on the difference in the growth rates of fixed capital, which reflects many years of underinvestment in Siberian machine-building in comparison with machine-building in the USSR as a whole.

[18]T. Baranova, "Osnovnye pokazateli razvitiia promyshlennosti Sibiri v sed'moi i deviatoi piatiletkakh," *Izvestiia Sibirskogo otdeleniia AN SSSR, seriia obshchestvennykh nauk*, no. 1, vypusk1, 1979, p. 30.
[19]*Sibir' v edinom narodnokhoziaistvennom komplekse*, p. 245; T. Baranova, "Osnovnye pokazateli razvitiia promyshlennosti Sibiri v desyatoi pyatiletke," *Izvestiia Sibirskogo otdeleniya AN SSSR, seriia obshchestvennych nauk*, no. 11, vypusk 3, 1982, p. 73.
[20]*Razvitie narodnogo khoziaistva Sibiri*, p. 235.
[21]L. Gramoteeva, *Effektivnost' territorial'noi organizatsii proizvodstva*, Moscow, Mysl', 1979, p. 143.

TABLE 16

COMPARISON OF GROWTH RATES OF INDUSTRIAL AND MACHINE-BUILDING OUTPUT IN THE USSR AND SIBERIA[22]

	USSR			Siberia		
	1961-65	1966-70	1971-75	1961-65	1966-70	1971-75
Average annual output growth (%)						
(a) Industry	8.6	8.4	7.4	8.6	9.4	8.2
(b) Machine-building	12.35	11.7	11.1	12.45	12.4	9.8
Ratio of (b) to (a)	1.44	1.39	1.58	1.44	1.32	1.19

TABLE 17

BASIC INDICATORS FOR MACHINE-BUILDING IN THE USSR AND SIBERIA, 1961-75 (%)[23]

		Average annual rates of growth	
	Output	Employment	Fixed Capital
USSR	11.5	4.85	12.2
Siberia	11.0	4.2	9.35

The lack of dynamism in Siberian machine-building is particularly manifested in the immobility of its regional structure, which has almost not changed during the past two decades. In West Siberia, which accounts for more than 70 percent of all Siberia's machine-building output, Novosibirsk oblast' as always provides the largest part of production growth. In East Siberia the major share of increments to output (about 75 percent) is traditionally supplied by Krasnoiarsk krai and Irkutsk oblast'.

---

[22] *Narkhoz SSSR v 1975*, pp. 190, 191, 255. *Narkhoz RSFSR v 1975*, pp. 47-49. *Ocherki ekonomiki Sibiri*, p. 276.
[23] *Ocherki ekonomiki Sibiri*, p. 281.

2. LACK OF CORRESPONDENCE OF THE STRUCTURE OF PRODUCTION TO REQUIREMENTS

Unlike the machine-building complex of western regions of the USSR, which have formed over decades and produce 90% of the country's machine-building output, Siberian machine-building has a very recent history. Its nucleus, formed during the war years, was composed of enterprises evacuated from western regions and their specialization was determined by the demands of war time.

In the post-war period the location and specialization of machine-building enterprises in Siberia, determined by branch ministries, was governed primarily by the interests of industrial branches. The economic structure of Siberia and the region's own requirements were given the lowest priority consideration. Therefore, first, the plants located in Siberia are extremely varied in the nature of their output, which reduces product specialization and technological cooperation within the region to a minimum. Second, the location and specialization of machine-building plants does not at all correspond to the extent of requirements for any given machine in Siberia. In other words, the structure of machine-building production in Siberia does not correspond to the structure of requirements; it does not meet the region's needs.

As a result of the fact that the output of the region's leading machine-building plants is oriented primarily toward the national market, and the list of machines and equipment produced does not coincide with the local economy's profile, the amount of machine-building products imported into Siberia is almost equal to the amount exported. And while for regions in the European zone of the USSR trade in machine-building products is characterized primarily by shipments within the zone, for Siberia it is just the opposite—less of its machine-building output ends up within the Eastern zone and more is shipped the European zone.

Using the example of West Siberia, let us examine the correspondence of the structure of heavy machine-building to the region's economic specialization and its role in overall USSR machine-building for basic types of products (see table 18).

TABLE 18

BRANCH STRUCTURE OF MACHINE-BUILDING IN THE USSR AND WEST SIBERIA (%)[24]

	Branch Structure USSR	Branch Structure West Siberia	West Siberia's share of USSR production
Machine-building (excluding metalworking and repair)	100	100	5.1
Energy and power MB	1.9	5.47	14.7
Electrical MB	12.0	13.3	5.7
Mining MB	1.77	3.71	10.7
Machine Tools	4.29	5.35	6.45
Automobile industry	11.54	3.8	1.64
Tractors & agricultural MB	11.0	17.5	8.2
Metallurgical MB	1.4	-	-
Oil and gas equipment	0.95	0.78	4.2
Construction equipment	2.06	0.68	1.7
Logging and paper MB	0.39	0.12	1.55
Construction materials MB	0.7	0.34	2.52
Chemical Industry MB	0.95	0.78	4.2
Hoisting-transporting MB	1.6	0.1	3.1
Total for 13 branches	51.4	52.0	5.17
Other branches	49.6	48.0	-

This table calls for the following comments. The relatively high share of mining machine-building, both with respect to the region and in the national context, would seem to be justified. Less warranted is the high share of agricultural machine-building since the share of all of Siberia in national agricultural production does not exceed 8 percent, and the share of machinetools—a very labor-intensive branch of machine-building—seems excessively high. But the shares of oil and gas MB, construction equipment, hoisting-transporting MB, chemical MB, and the automobile industry are in sharp contradiction to the requirements of West Siberia. Let us examine several examples characterizing the balance of production and consumption of machine-building products in Siberia. The share of West Siberia in national production of electric power is 7%, while the share of energy and power

[24]G. Kurbatova, "Mashinostroenie," in *Ocherki ekonomiki Sibiri*, p. 278.

machine-building is about 15%. However, Siberia's requirements for energy and power machine-building products are 60-65% covered by imports from other, primarily western, regions of the country.[25] At the same time, the lion's share of the output of plants located in the region are shipped to the west. Siberia produces about 9% of all metal in the USSR, but metallurgical equipment is almost not produced there. Siberia is a region of open-pit mining work, but as yet there is not one plant producing excavators in Siberia (or, incidentally, in the Far East or Kazakhstan).

Of course, interregional ties for machine-building are an entirely normal phenomenon for the economy of a huge country. But a most important factor for Siberia comes into play here—the severe labor shortage. Machine-building is in general the most labor-intensive branch of industry. In Siberia machinery's share of industrial production is about 21-23% and its share of the industrial workforce is about 35%.[26] And a situation in which Siberia, experiencing a severe labor shortage (especially of skilled labor, which is chiefly used in machine-building), produces machinery and equipment that is for the-most part (90-100% for some items) shipped to regions with much more favorable labor balances, must be considered pathological. And at the same time almost 80% of its own requirements (85% for East Siberia and 73% for West Siberia) are satisfied by imports.[27] Here we must keep in mind that massive transcontinental shipments of large-unit, difficult to transport equipment creates special problems for the country's transportation system, which is already overburdened with spontaneously growing shipments of raw materials and fuel on a broad scale. And we may note that the basic load falls on the railroad system whose critical condition is well known.

3. HYPOTHESIS ON THE DEVELOPMENT OF SIBERIAN MACHINE-BUILDING

As long as Siberia maintains a 6% share of machine-building production and ships in 80% of its equipment requirements, largely from the European part of the country, it is unrealistic to count on dynamic development of its economy and the opening up of its vast unsettled and inaccessible areas. And this relates not only to economic but to social development: the location of machine-building there helps to retain the labor force, to prevent its migration to other regions. Developing only extractive industry will not solve these problems.

[25] *Ocherki ekonomiki Sibiri*, pp. 278, 279.
[26] *Sibir' v edinom narodnokhoziaistvennom komplekse*, pp. 36, 182.
[27] Ibid., p. 183.

At present, the prevailing notion is that regions in southern Siberia should remain the zone of intensive development of machine-building, while it is absolutely inexpedient to locate machine-building enterprises in the northern regions. According to this conception, the southern part of central Siberia should become the center of energy and power MB, hoisting and transporting MB, construction equipment, metallurgical MB, mining, coal, oil, and gas machinery and equipment.

The particular difficulty in developing Siberian machine-building, thus, is the need to simultaneously increase the rates of output growth and sharply restructure the branch composition of production, changing the specialization of machine-building enterprises. According to the calculations of the Institute of Economics of Industry of the USSR Academy of Science, the growth rate should be 11-12%, while currently it is apparently less than 8%. And in order not only to halt the sharp decline in Siberian machine-building growth rates but shift to the opposite trend, very large-scale investments will be necessary. The restructuring of production to bring the specialization of Siberian machine-building enterprises into line with the region's economic specialization is possible only by the massive reconstruction and modernization of these enterprises. But all the difficulties and contradictions of industrial reconstruction[28] are redoubled in Siberia. We will note one other important factor: the share of construction work in industrial investment in Siberia is substantially higher than in most other regions of the USSR, i.e., the share of investment in industrial structures is higher and the share of investment in equipment is correspondingly lower. The difficulties of construction work in Siberia are aggravated by several specific factors that are examined in the next chapter. Thus, the intensification of the development of Siberian machine-building and bringing it closer to the region's needs requires diverting investment resources for these purposes of a magnitude that is impossible given the country's current economic situation as long as existing economic and political priorities are maintained.

Thus, will the stagnant condition of Siberian machine-building continue in the 1980's? Who might accelerate its development? What could influence the leaders of the Soviet economy and spur them into accelerated investment in the construction of new and reconstruction of existing machine-building enterprises in Siberia in actuality and not just on paper?

---

[28]See B. Rumer, "Soviet Investment Policy: Unresolved Problems." *Problems of Communism*, September-October, 1982.

The extent of investment activity aimed at the development of Siberia's machine-building and its spatial orientation depends on the general idea on which the formation of Siberia's economy is based and on the character of the planned development of the region.

In this context, it seems that the following alternatives should be examined:

1) the purposeful comprehensive development of Siberia in the broadest sense, determined by the geopolitical situation in that part of Asia. For this it is necessary to create conditions that would retain the population and counteract its outflow. From this point of view, the creation of a balanced structure of the economy in developing regions, with elements of autarchy, is a fundamental factor. And such a structure is unthinkable without sufficiently developed machine-building. And this means not only heavy machine-building to satisfy the requirements of the extractive branches, and not only service-type machine-building (repair enterprises, etc.), but also instrument making and, in general, machinery enterprises of varied specialization must be placed in Siberia based on a concept of planned proportional development of the region. The military-strategic interests of the USSR, requiring deconcentration of machine-building as the leading branch of defense industry, also coincide with this conception. The expansion of machine-building capacity primarily in the Novosibirsk-Krasnoiarsk zone where the primary part of Siberia's machine-building is already concentrated contradicts the logic of locating enterprises from the standpoint of military-economic planning.

2) the more narrow approach to developing Siberia oriented toward the extraction and primary processing of raw materials and fuel resources, determined as before by narrow branch interests with Siberia's role subordinate to and specialized for national interests. It would seem appropriate to call this attitude toward the development of Siberian economy "consumerism" from the standpoint of central planning organizations. Precisely this second alternative dominates in planning calculations and projections, which outline the creation of the largest center of heavy and power machine-building of the Asiatic part of the country in the southern latitudinal belt—the soft underbelly of Siberia.

Such a position is based on objective prerequisites. The major one is the proposed availability of surplus and cheap electric power there in connection with the development of the Kansk-Achinsk fuel-energy complex (as shown above, this prerequisite is being realized very slowly). Furthermore, a powerful production potential has already been created here, concentrating almost half of the fixed capital and labor resources in machine-building east of the Urals. And her important advantages—the center of Siberian metallurgy is here, transportation conditions are, by Siberian standards, most favorable, the infrastructure and the availability of skilled machine-building workers are, again by Siberian standards, developed—make this zone of Siberia the most attractive in an economic sense for the massive development of machine-building. Nonetheless, while arguments of a strategic nature are examined in the theoretical works, for pragmatists of Soviet planning concerned only about today, they remain ideas cut off from practice.

The development of heavy machine-building in the southern part of West Siberia should, in the opinion of Soviet planners and scientists, be a favored by other important advantages:
—the sharp increase in the requirements for its output in the adjacent regions of Siberia and Kazakhstan; —the exceptional unmatched position of the region with regard to the possibility of introducing new electric power-intensive technology, in particular shifting to electric power for smelting, heating, welding, and heat treating metals; —possibilities, incomparable with any other region in the country, for reducing labor expenditures (which is so important precisely for Siberia) by raising the amount of power per worker; —proximity to the primary metallurgical base of the Asiatic part of the USSR—Kuznets and West Siberian metallurgical plants; —the availability of skilled labor; —the most developed (under Siberian conditions) transportation network.

We may divide the listed factors into two groups those of an economic-geographic nature and those that depend on the rate and scale of realization of the Kansk-Achinsk power project. And while factors in the first group objectively exist, those in the second group, for reasons laid out above, put off the realization of plans for the development of a heavy machine-building center in southern Siberia to an undetermined time.

But dragging this problem out has serious consequences not only for the economic development of Siberia but for the entire Asiatic part of the USSR (especially Kazakhstan and the Far East), which, according to the idea embodied in long-range plans, should receive many necessary types of machinery and equipment from the machine-building industry of the southern zone of West Siberia.

Table 19 provides an impression of how great the difference is in machine-building production between the European part of the USSR (including the Urals) and the Asiatic part. Analysis of this table shows the importance of creating a powerful machine-building base in the eastern part of the country.

Special attention should be paid to the correlation in repair work, from which it is clear how much more worn out the stock of machinery and equipment is in Asiatic regions of the USSR than in European regions. And from this it follows that the share of replacement in investment in machine-building in Asiatic regions must be higher (possibly twice as high) than in European regions. Thus, much larger investments are required per unit of net increase in machine-building capacity in Asiatic regions.

TABLE 19

DISTRIBUTION OF MACHINE-BUILDING IN THE EUROPEAN (INCLUDING THE URALS) AND ASIATIC PART OF THE USSR (%)[29]

Branch	Gross Output		Employment		Fixed Capital	
	European	Asiatic	European	Asiatic	European	Asiatic
Machine-building and metalworking	86.7	13.3	86.1	13.9	86.0	14.0
of which, machinebuilding:	88.0	11.2	88.4	11.6	85.0	15.0
Heavy, power and transportation MB	89.4	10.6	89.1	10.9	88.3	11.7
Chemical and oil MB	91.1	8.9	91.1	8.9	89.7	10.3
Light and Food Industry MB	91.7	8.3	92.5	7.5	91.7	8.3
Automobile industry	96.9	3.1	96.2	3.8	96.4	3.6
Tractors and agricultural MB	84.0	16.0	82.5	17.5	81.2	18.8
Electrical industry MB	84.8	15.2	85.6	14.4	84.8	15.2
Machine tools; tools and dies	89.1	10.9	89.1	10.9	88.4	11.6
Instruments	95.3	4.7	94.4	5.6	91.6	8.4
General machine-building	99.1	0.9	98.6	1.4	98.2	1.8
Other branches of machine-building	94.0	6.0	94.8	5.2	96.4	3.6
Metal wares and metal structures	83.4	13.6	86.2	13.8	80.0	20.0
Repair	72.3	27.7	73.9	26.1	70.5	29.5

In examining table 19, it must be kept in mind that the center of gravity of the consumption of power, transportation, chemical, oil, and several other types of machinery in the country is shifting rapidly to the east.

4. SOME SPECIAL DEMANDS ON SIBERIAN MACHINE-BUILDING PRODUCTION

The task of creating a machine-building base for developing Siberia's resources has a qualitative as well as quantitative aspect: Siberia's natural conditions and the unique scale of mineral resources

---

[29] V. Evstigneev, *Effektivnost' razmeshcheniia mashinostroeniia v vostochnykh i zapadnykh raionakh SSSR*, Moscow, Nauka, 1972, p. 58.

necessitate the production of machinery and equipment that is specially suited to these conditions. Developing the oil and gas deposits of West Siberia requires creating and producing equipment for the simultaneous but separate working of two or three strata, highly efficent pumps, and automated drilling installations that are easily erected.

Working Siberia's large coal deposits within the foreseeable future is impossible without using special powerful complexes for stripping operations and the corresponding transportation technology (rotor excavators, walking excavator-draglines, self-propelled scrappers for layer stripping, coal-carrying trucks), cutting, cleaning, and drilling equipment, and mechanisms with high unit capacity and productivity.

For thermal powerplants operating on Kansk-Achinsk coal, special boilers suitable for processing the specific brown coals of this basin are needed as well as a system for ash processing and disposal.

The huge volume of construction requires highly efficient bulldozers, trench excavators, various types of cranes with high capacity and reach, and other special-use construction equipment adapted for local operating conditions.

Transportation machine-building is given a special role. Primarily due to their inaccessibility to transport, many deposits such as, for example, Udokansk copper, Gorevsk lead and zinc, Deputatsk tin ore, Molodezhnyi chrysolite-asbestos, Zhirekenskii and Orekitkanskii molybdenum, and other no less important deposits are in a preserved condition. Transportation expenditures in regions of West Siberia where oil and gas sites are undergoing initial industrial development amount to 30-50% of production expenditures,[30] and as work shifts farther north in Tiumensk oblast' their share grows still more. In northern regions of Siberia where the landscape is characterized by huge areas of swampy tundra and a large number of water barriers, special hydrofoil-type transportation and snow and swamp caterpillars with heavy freight and long-range capabilities are needed.

Thus, the problem is not simply to increase the volume of production of machinery and equipment in line with Siberia's huge and growing requirements but to create and produce special equipment, in many cases on a fundamentally new basis. By simply adapting existing models, created for operation under ordinary conditions, to Siberian conditions, the accelerated development of Siberia's fuel, power, and raw material resources will be impossible.

---

[30] *Sabir' v edinom narodnokhoziaistvennom komplekse*, p. 181.

Is Soviet machine-building, given its current production capacities and its contemporary technical level, able to cope with meeting the requirements for reliable equipment with parameters that are oriented toward the regional conditions of operation in Siberia? Apparently not. The point is not only the decline in production of the majority of types of equipment mentioned but in the reduced pace of creation of new types of this equipment. Thus, according to Soviet statistics, in the second half of the 1970's the number of new models of machinery and equipment fell in comparison with the first half of the decade for power, electrotechnical mining, pump-compressor, casting, hoisting-transporting, transportation, and construction materials industry machinery.[31]

The gap between the capabilities of Soviet machine-building and the requirements of Siberia's fuel-energy complex are increasing and will increase more rapidly as investment in the fuel-energy branches outpaces investment in machine-building.

* * *

It would, however, be incorrect to suppose that this problem does not worry the leaders of Soviet planning and its theoreticians or that significant efforts are not being taken to solve it. Judging from publications in recent years,[32] the idea of creating a nucleus of heavy machine-building for eastern regions of the USSR in the southern part of West Siberia is finding more and more proponents among representatives of the economic and scientific-administrative establishment and is receiving support in long-range plans and schemes of the development and location of industry in the period up to the year 2000. There is evidence of a growing conflict of interests surrounding this question between such scientific and economic organizations as the USSR Gosplan's Council for the Study of the Productive Forces, the Institute of Economics and the Institute of Economics and Organization of Industrial Production of the USSR Academy of Science, and Siberian regional party committees, on the one hand, which press for increasing the investment quota of Siberian machine-building by limiting investment in machine-building in western regions, and branch ministries, on the other hand, that stubbornly prefer to invest in the existing machine-building structures of the Central, North-West, Ukrainian, Volga, and Ural regions. We have no information revealing the position of Gosplan or, more important, the Military-Industrial Commission of the USSR Council of Ministers. It is possible that their position on

---

[31] *Narkhoz SSSR v 1980*, pp. 100-101.
[32] See, for example, *Planovoe khoziaistvo*, no. 3, 1980, p. 35.

this contradictory question has still not been formulated in final form. Nonetheless, an analysis of the literature gives the impression that the flow of investment to Siberian machine-building became more intensive in the second half of the 1970s, and we are inclined to believe that this tendency will increase. A change in the course of concentrating machine-building in western regions of the country and overcoming an inertia in the location of this branch that has formed over many decades requires great and purposeful efforts on the part of the Soviet leadership. Equalizing the disproportion in the development of Siberian machine-building is a process that is complex both with respect to resources and technology. The decisive factor for stimulating its acceleration is the implementation of the Kansk-Achinsk energy project.

* * * * *

The evaluation of the prospects for industrial development of Siberia and for implementation of ambitious investment programs adopted for the region does not make any sense if the capabilities of its construction industry are not examined. Rather than going into an all-encompassing analysis of this sphere of the Soviet economy let us focus our attention on the most important factors hampering construction in Siberia. This will be the topic of the next chapter.

CHAPTER SIX

PECULIARITIES OF CONSTRUCTION IN SIBERIA

> Increasing the scale of investment activity is mainly hindered by the retardation—which moreover is intensifying—of the construction base (the capacities of construction enterprises and enterprises which produce construction materials) .... [The] share of capital investments in the construction base in Siberia is 20-25 percent lower than in the country as a whole. For this reason, Siberian investments are absorbed more slowly than those in the European part of the country, and there is a much larger backlog of unfinished construction work ....
> The absence of the necessary construction base is perhaps the main reason why the installation of objects drags out in Siberia, and why it takes so long to put them into exploitation. What is more, some of them drop out of the list of new construction projects entirely for the above-mentioned reason.
>
> Prof. Boris Orlov, 1980

Investment programs planned and implemented within Siberia are so varied in their technological specifics and in the conditions under which they are carried out that there is no sense in examining, as an object of analysis, a single Siberian construction complex. While construction conditions in regions along the Trans-Siberian Railroad essentially do not differ from average conditions for the country, construction in the higher latitudes of Siberia has special features. Investment activity and construction-installation work in Siberia is rather rapidly shifting to the north, to extreme conditions. Thus, the share of construction north of the polar circle in West Siberia increased from 16 percent to 33 percent between 1965 and 1975.[1] Data presented in the report on the first phase of this project characterizing the regional shift in investment activity in 1976-80 and the growth of investment in the oil and gas complex lanned for 1981-85 provide a basis for concluding that by the end of the current decade this share will be around 50%. Therefore, we will focus attention on the problems of construction in the northern regions of Siberia, especially in the northern part of Tiumen oblast where investment activity and the concentration of construction-installation work will be highest not only on the scale of Siberia but for the entire country.

---

[1] *EKO*, no. 4, 1981, p. 75.

We will try to formulate briefly the basic characteristics of construction in Siberia.

The first of them was just mentioned: the essential dissimilarity of all parameters of the construction process in the north and south of the region. Such regions of southern and central Siberia as Kuzbass-Altai (Kemerovo and Novosibirsk oblast and Altai krai) or the Irkutsk-Angara industrial agglomeration have mature production structures with a rather developed construction base. A large part of Siberia's production of construction materials is also concentrated in these regions (93% of cement, 60% of reinforced concrete)[2] as well as the largest construction organizations, which formed in the process of constructing large hydroelectric stations. Therefore it is not at all correct to extend the idea of difficulties of construction in Siberia to these regions. Thus, a particular feature of Siberian construction is the growing spatial gap between the concentration of investment in a northern direction and the developing construction base in the south.

A second feature is that the territory is as yet unsettled. The investment program there must be of a pioneering nature. In addition to productive construction, the transportation network, productive and social infrastructures must be newly created.

A third feature is the deconcentration of many small-scale construction projects as the oil and gas deposits of West Siberia are developed across a vast area: the level of capital investment per hectare for the majority of projects does not exceed 0.5 million rubles, while in the constructin of machine-building enterprises in sourthen Siberia it is more than 10 million rubles per hectare.[3] To this must be added the uncertainty about key parameters of the oil-gas investment program, which depend on the exploration for reserves. All this gives rise to special demands for high maneuverability and mobility of construction work.

A fourth feature is the extremely severe natural and climatic conditions: the eternal permafrost, seismic activity, swampiness, and low winter temperatures, all of which affects design decisions and construction equipment and technology.

The listed factors dictate the need, first, to invest initially in the creation of a construction base and the development of the production of construction materials and structures in regions where construction will be concentrated; second, to better equip construction with the appropriate construction technology and vehicles; third, to carry out construction projects with due regard to natural and climatic conditions;

[2] *EKO*, no. 12, 1980, p. 30.
[3] *Sibir' v edinom narodnokhoziaistvennom komplekse*, p. 201.

fourth, to use building materials that are most appropriate for the natural and technological conditions of the construction project; and, fifth, to create an organizational form of construction that would be mobile and sufficiently universal in a technological sense. Let us examine how these demands are realized in practice.

1. UNDERINVESTMENT IN SIBERIA'S CONSTRUCTION INDUSTRY

According to the very cautious estimates of Soviet experts, implementing the planned investment program in Siberia will require doubling the amount of construction work in the region. The first condition that must be met is the creation and rapid development of the corresponding construction base and the production of construction materials and structures. One of the axioms of the theory of Soviet planning is the rule that the growth of investment in the construction base in developing regions must be more rapid than the growth of investment in the economy of the region as a whole and must be proportional to the planned acceleration of construction-assembly work. From this it follows that the capacity of production facilities supplying bulding materials and services to construction must develop at rates that exceed the rate of increase in construction-assembly work. For Siberia as a whole, this difference in rates should be 150-200 percent, but in fact it is 110-120 percent.[4] It is also perfectly obvious that the share of investment in the construction industry as a whole, including the construction materials industry and construction structures, as a percentage of total capital investment should be substantially higher in the Siberian regions of pioneering development than in the USSR as a whole or the RSFSR. However, factual data reflect just the opposite picture.

TABLE 20

INVESTMENT IN THE CONSTRUCTION INDUSTRY AS A SHARE OF TOTAL CAPITAL INVESTMENT[5]

Region	1971	1972	1973	1974	1975
RSFSR	4.0	4.1	4.2	4.1	4.4
Siberia	3.0	2.7	2.3	2.5	2.7
West Siberia	3.4	2.8	2.2	2.5	2.6
East Siberia	2.5	2.6	2.4	2.5	2.8

[4] *Dolgosrochnye programmy kapital'nykh vlozhenii,* Moscow, *Ekonomika,* 1976, p. 134.
[5] *Sibir' v edinom narodnokhoziaistvennom komplekse,* p. 203.

As table 20 shows, the share of investment in the construction industry in Siberia was, first, lower than for the RSFSR as a whole, and, second, while this share was growing for the RSFSR, for Siberia (and what is most notable, for West Siberia) it was declining. Investment in the construction materials industry as a share of total capital investment in Siberia declined during 1971-75 from 0.91 percent to 0.88 percent, and for West Siberia from 0.74 percent to 0.56 percent.[6] As a result the production of construction materials and the growth of the construction base in general lagged farther behind the planned rates. This lag is characteristics of the construction complex of the country as a whole, but in Siberia (especially West Siberia) it is much more clearly evident.

Still more significant is the disproportion within the construction complex itself: construction work is not very intensive, but it is developing nonetheless, while at the same time its base—the construction materials industry—is stagnating. The trend in fixed capital put in place is convincing evidence of this. While annual fixed capital put in place in construction increased from 234 to 300 million rubles between 1971 and 1975 in Siberia as a whole, including a gain from 162 to 185 million rubles in West Siberia, fixed capital put in place in the construction materials industry in Siberia declined during this period from 85 to 69 million rubles for all of Siberia and from 47 to 27 million rubles for West Siberia.[7]

According to estimates by Soviet specialists, the share of investment in the material-technical base of construction in the developed regions of Siberia should be 3-4% of total investment in the economy, and in newly developing regions (which includes, first of all, the northern territory of Tiumen oblast) it should be 10%.[8] Thus, the actual value of this indicator (see table 20) is much lower than what is needed, and all the troubles of the region's construction sphere center around this lag, this disproportion.

2. THE ABSENCE OF CONSTRUCTION TECHNOLOGY AND DESIGNS THAT MEET THE EXTREME CONDITIONS OF CONSTRUCTION ON NORTHERN REGIONS OF SIBERIA

A direct consequence of the insufficient investment in Siberia's construction complex is the low technological level of construction organizations. West Siberian construction organizations have 22 kopecks of fixed productive capital per ruble of construction-assembly

---
[6]Loc. cit.
[7]Ibid., p. 204.
[8]V. Bogachev, "Osobennosti investitsionnykh program osvoeniia Sibiri," in *Dolgosrochnye programmy kapital'nykh vlozhenii*, p. 134.

work,[9] while the average for the USSR is 34 kopecks. The low level of capitalization of construction in Siberia must be viewed together with the severe shortage of labor.

But more important is the fact that machinery and equipment operated in the northern regions of Siberia must meet the demands of natural and climatic conditions. In the severe Siberian climate, construction equipment wears out faster and breaks down more often than in other regions. In the north of West Siberia automobiles, tractors, bulldozers, and scrapers last for only 30-35% of their normal service lives.[10] Idle time is extremely high due to breakdowns and accidents. But even equipment in good repair is used with low productivity. For example, the work rate of excavators in Yakutia in winter is reduced by 40%. The reason is that the stock of construction and road-building machinery is absolutely not suited to conditions in the north due to the low cold-resistance of metal used in machine-building, the rapid wearing out of moving parts, the lack of suitable low-temperature engine starters, operator cabin construction that is inappropriate for normal conditions of operation in the north, etc.

Maintaining ordinary equipment under conditions for the north requires strengthening buildings—modernizing, winter-proofing, additional heating and lighting—and this must be done before machinery is put into operation. However, such work is not done in the majority of cases.

The reliability of ordinary equipment drops sharply under the influence of low temperatures, and the amount of repair work and expenditures on spare parts grow. While repair expenditures grow sharply, the repair base of construction organizations in Siberia and its equipment is at a low level of development; the quality of repair is correspondingly lower, much lower, than at similar sites in the country's middle zone. Practically all construction organizations manufacture many types of spare parts for their equipment themselves.

Conditions of the Siberian north make it expedient to use machinery and equipment with a higher unit capacity intended for low temperatures, permanently frozen ground, and swampy land. However, paradoxically, the share of such machinery in the stock of construction road-building, and other equipment in northern Siberia is lower than in the country as a whole. And it should be noted here that in general the production of large-capacity construction machines in the USSR comprises a small share of the production of construction equipment. For example, 250-hp bulldozers comprised only 1% of total bulldozer

---

[9]Ibid., p. 139.
[10]*Ekonomicheskie problemy razvitiia Sibiri*, Novosibirsk, Nauka, 1974.

production in the mid-1970's and more powerful models were not even produced.[11] The main factor hindering the production of special equipment for the north is not insufficient attention to the problem on the whole and not a lack of ideas from scientific and design work. Many models of machinery for northern use have been created in Soviet scientific and design organizations. The main obstacles are a lack of production capacity in machine-building for serial production of these models and a shortage of highly cold-resistant steel. The first factor was discussed above. Therefore, we will look briefly only at the second.

Soviet operational experience and experiments conducted by specialists in the northern regions shows that parts made of steel and iron in serially produced automobiles, tractors, and construction machines have a tendency to shattter due to brittleness when subject to blows or overloading under operating temperatures below 40° C. In northern regions of Siberia the temperature in winter gets down to 60° C, and quite often when winds are high. Under such low temperatures the tensile strength of steel falls and in certain temperature intervals, depending on the load conditions, steel frequently becomes brittle and it is then possible for machinery parts to shatter, even under loads that are less than nominally permissible. Therefore, under such climatic conditions special cold-resistant steel alloys with high tensile strength are needed, but the production of such steel, like the production of heat-strengthened rolled metal is in a completely insufficient level. It is precisely this steel that the USSR imports from Japan and West Germany, and the import possibilities are very limited. Therefore, there are no grounds for optimism in evaluating the possibilities for increasing the production of construction and transport equipment for northern use in the USSR in the forseeable future. And it is hardly likely that imports of low-alloy steel will increase substantially.

In addition, the difficulties with developing and producing special tires, gasoline and diesel fuel for use in the north, northern types of motor oil and lubricants, etc. should be mentioned. These technologies are lagging greatly in the USSR and Western help is needed here also.

But in order to implement construction programs in Siberia not only special technology but also construction designs adapted to the extreme conditions are needed. It should be noted above all that standard designs are used extremely widely in housing and productive construction in the USSR. In the mid-1970's the share of construction

---

[11] E. Kushchev, "Osnovnye napravleniia i organizatsiia rabot po sozdaniiu tekhniki dlia Severa," *Problemy Severa*, vol. 19, *Problemy povysheniia effektivnosti stroitel'stva na Severe*, Moscow, Nauka, 1974, pp. 187, 188.

using standard designs was 81% for the country as a whole.[12] The goal in creating and using designs on a mass basis is to economize on resources, struggle with wastefulness, and discipline both clients and contractors. The practice of standard design is the only means of limiting the exaggeration of estimated construction costs. However, the striving for standardization in any and all types of construction has gone beyond all rational limits and turned into "stencil-construction." Siberian cities are built primarily with exactly the same standard buildings as are constructed in western and southern regions of the country. The same relates to industrial construction.

As far we know, the only, or at least one of very few, standard design for residential buildings in regions beyond the polar circle was developed and introduced in Norilsk when the director of the Norilsk Combine and, hence, the city's boss was current candidate member of the Politburo, Vladimir Dolgikh. But between the polar circle zone of Siberia and, say, the foothills of Altai or the Minusinsk hollow, there is a vast territory with diverse natural and climatic conditions. And the construction of production structures and social infrastructure projects in these areas is based on one or two standard designs. It is shocking but a fact that in buildings erected in Siberia wood is used just as sparingly as in the steppe regions of the Ukraine. And this is a consequence of the excessive standardization of designs.

It is impossible to understand or explain the existing construction practice in Siberia without dealing with at least the basic factors determining the level and character of the contemporary stage of development of the Soviet construction industry as a whole.

3. RETARDATION OF DESIGN AND INDUSTRIAL CONSTRUCTION TECHNOLOGY IN THE USSR

A fundamental factor hindering the realization of Soviet investment plans, including investment programs in Siberia, is the obsolescence of design principles and methods of erecting buildings and structures and the incompatibility of construction technology with the tasks that it faces. We will try to analyze briefly the factors underlying this phenomenon.

During the years of its existence the Soviet construction industry has experienced two revolutions: 1) the construction boom of industrialization in the 1930's (the rejection of seasonal construction work and the introduction of hoisting—transporting equipment into

---

[12] *Metody i praktika opredeleniia effektivnosti kapital'nykh vlozhenii i novoi tekhniki*, no. 26, Moscow, Nauka, 1976, p. 76. V. Krasovskii, "Investitsionnyi kompleks," *Voprosy ekonomiki*, no. 1, 1979, p. 62.

construction), and 2) the second half of the 1950's—the Khrushchev housing construction explosion (the transition to the production line, completely prefabricated construction). In both the first and the second instance a radical change in construction technology gave rise to a sharp increase in labor productivity: both in the 1930's and in the second half of the 1950's the rate of growth of labor productivity increased and amounted to about 9%.[13]

Beginning in 1966 the rate of growth of labor productivity in construction has exhibited a steady downward trend and has lagged behind the analogous indicator for industry. It would seem that the renewal of fixed capital that has taken place at a more rapid rate in construction than in other branches of the economy (fixed capital in construction in 1980 was 256% above the 1970 level, while in industry this figure was 216% and in agriculture 225%)[14] should have averted this tendency. But this did not happen and the reason apparently is that the increase in fixed capital involved the extensive development of the traditional technological base of construction and not the introduction of new technology.

In the 1970s the average annual growth rate of labor productivity was 3.6%, and in the last three years of the decade (1978-80) it fell to 0.7%.[15] In other words, the growth of labor productivity in construction almost ceased at the beginning of the 1980s. If we add to this the fact that employment in construction has almost not grown in this period (an average annual increase of 0.5%), the need for a radical overhaul of construction technology in the USSR becomes obvious.

The revolution in the construction industry's technology in the USSR in the 1950s was due to an unprecedented jump in housing construction in the first five years of the Khrushchev period. Investment in housing construction increased by more than 400% during 1950-1960. Its share in the total volume of investment in the national economy jumped from 19.5% to 25.1% in only three years (1956-58).[16] Thanks to these efforts a record increase in construction output for the entire postwar history of the USSR was achieved in 1956-60 (about 90%), and the amount of new housing introduced during that five-year period

---

[13] *Kapital'noe stroitel'stvo v SSSR: statisticheskii sbornik*, Moscow, Gosstatizdat, 1961, p. 252.
[14] *Narkhoz SSSR v 1980*, p. 50.
[15] Ibid., p. 351.
[16] It is appropriate to compare with 1970-80 when capital investment in housing construction increased by only 33 percent, its share in 1980 was 13.4 percent, and the amount of housing introduced in 1975-80 decreased by 2 percent.

increased by almost 250%.[17]

But the implementation of this investment program was possible only because of the massive introduction of prefabricated concrete in construction, the unification of construction components it provided, and the sharp increase in the share of factory-produced components that are merely put in place on the construction site. This was the essence of the construction revolution in the USSR, for which a new branch—the production of prefabricated reinforced concrete—was actually created. This in turn required a significant increase in the production of cement and metal. During the decade 1950-1960 the production of cement increased by 447%, steel by 240%, and prefabricated concrete by 2500%.[18] However, after 1965 the effect resulting from the mass use of prefabricated concrete technology diminished.

Here is the opinion on this of authoritative Soviet experts:

> From the moment of enactment of the decree of the Central Committee of the CPSU and the USSR Council of Ministers on the production of prefabricated concrete, its output increased more than 20 times, exceeding the level of production in the U.S., France and the West Germany taken together. As the branch fully absorbed constructions of prefabricated concrete, the increase in technical-economic indicators declined, and by now the orientation toward further expansion of the use of prefabricated concrete contradicts the requirements of scientific and technical progress.
>
> Moreover, a tendency is now observed toward heavier prefabricated protective constructions for buildings and structures, which leads to heavier supporting structures and, hence, to higher material-intensiveness and, above all, metal-intensiveness of construction. As a result the prime cost and labor intensity of construction are growing.[19]

The expansion of the production of reinforced concrete and its broader use to the point of replacing other types of construction materials everywhere went beyond the optimal boundaries already in the second half of the 1960s and is now in contradiction with technical progress in the design and erection of buildings and structures. This contradiction has increased with the growing volume of construction in the northeast, in unsettled regions with extreme natural and climatic conditions where special principles of design for industrial enterprises

---

[17] *Kapital'noe stroitel'stvo v SSSR*, pp. 57, 189.

[18] *Promyshlennost' SSSR: statisticheskii sbornik*, Moscow, Statistika, 1964, p. 164. *Kapital'noe stroitel'stvo v SSSR*, p. 242.

[19] E. Golland and S. Finkel', "Nekotorye problemy povysheniia effektivnosti stroitel'nogo kompleksa," *Izvestiia Sibirskogo otdeleniia AN SSSR, seriia obshchestvennykh nauk*, no. 1, vypusk 1, 1982.

and objects of the infrastructure are needed as well as construction components and materials that are suitable for these conditions. Let us examine briefly the essence of this contradiction. For this we will compare the real state of affairs in the USSR with the modern level of technological progress in design and construction of production structures, which the Soviet Union must attain if it is to cary out its ambitious investment program.

In Soviet design practice to date, primary attention is devoted to durability, to creating long-lasting production buildings. Under these conditions the tendency toward heavier prefabricated components for buildings and structures becomes more and more noticeable, and as a result the relative expenditure of cement, metal, and other materials grows, labor expenditures increase, construction times stretch out, and the subsequent reconstruction and modernization of enterprises is made more complex and more expensive.

The main idea of modern industrial construction is the transition from multipurpose to functional, inexpensive, and easily dismantled buildings, maximally adapted to the demands of specific technological processes. Their service life is substantially reduced and approaches the service life of the basic technological equipment. Thus, excess durability of structures is excluded and construction time is shortened.

One of the basic principles of modern design for industrial enterprises is the convertibility of new enterprises—creating the possibility for a transition from an old to a new technological scheme. The rapid replacement of models and the constant renewal of the assortment of goods produced generates a demand for movable equipment installations and the possibility of assembling equipment and productive structures from standard units. The practice of creating "flexible shops" and enterprises that can, without special difficulty, expand or retool to produce a new product has been widely developed in advanced industrial countries.

In such enterprises a system of bridge cranes as the main intrashop and intraplant means of transport loses its significance. Crane operation requires the construction of massive walls and supports designed for heavy loads. Characteristic of a "flexible shop" are widely developed floor transportation, conveyer systems, pneumatic transportation, and other means that create the possibility for varied and mobile transport schemes. It is important to note that rejecting the traditional use of bridge cranes leads to a reduction by several times in construction height and in overall weight of the components of industrial buildings.

The idea of the "flexible shop" has been widely introduced in machine-building and in light industry. This principle is especially important in military industry and, above all, in such branches as rocket construction, instrument building, and electronics where the possibility of a rapid transition from one type of product to another is of decisive significance.

In branches of industry such as metallurgy, chemicals, and cement where the basic technological equiment is in large stationary units, technical progress in construction is manifested not in the creation of "flexible" shops but in the use of lighter, less massive buildings.

Against the background of these modern trends, the design of industrial buildings in the USSR appears absolutely anachronistic. The obsoleteness of construction methods is manifested primarily in the wide use of bridge cranes as intraplant transportation and the absolutely insufficient use of floor transport or light suspended hoisting-transporting apparatus. For the majority of branches of industry, industrial buildings are designed and constructed to be equipped with bridge cranes. According to data of the Central Institute of Industrial Buildings (in Moscow), about 60% of all shops are equipped wth bridge cranes.[20]

The use of light constructions in such shops yields an insignificant effect. Characteristically for Soviet industry, an increase in unit capacity of equipment means an increase in weight and unit size, which in turn requires cranes of larger freight capacity and presupposes increased demands on the size of industrial buildings and the weight and capacity of structures. Bridge cranes widely used in Soviet plants have a capacity of 200-300 tons, and in oxygen-converter shops 450 tons. At a plant producing equipment for nuclear power stations (*Atommash*), the capacity of bridge cranes reaches 1,200 tons.

According to Soviet standards, if there is a bridge crane in a shop, even one of lowest capacity, the height of the structure can not be less than 8.4 meters, even if the height of equipment does not exceed 1-2 meters. All the rest of the heated, lighted, and ventilated building space is nothing other than the zone of movement for the bridge crane.

In modern industrial buildings of Soviet enterprises equipped with bridge cranes, the size and mass of columns, foundations, and beams is more than two-thirds dependent on crane loads.

It would seem that under such circumstances designers should make strict calculations in the choice of bridge crane capacity and strive to limit it as much as possible. However, in practice the design of crane capacity is based on the maximum possible mass of technological loads. The number of cranes is determined not by the volume of work but by obsolete standards for installing a unit of hauling equipment per 60 meters of hauling distance.

[20] *EKO*, no. 9, 1980, p. 15.

Planning and design decisions on the part of construction for modern Soviet industrial buildings depend much more on the type of bridge crane adopted in the design than on the technology of production. For example, structures of shops producing enamelled pots and pans that weigh no more than 2-3 kilograms differ very little in scale and weight from those of a rolled metal shop in a metallurgical plants. The construction of carcasses of electric powerplants is just as hevy as in the casting and other shops of machine-building enterprises producing very heavy products.

In addition to the excessive increase in bridge cranes, many other obstacles lie in the path of creating more efficient construction designs. One of them, for example, is strict standards for the "span" of arrangements of technological equipment, which leads to the incomplete use of production floor space and building volume and to a significant lengthening of transport, power, and communication lines.

A leading Gosplan expert notes in this regard: "No one would get the idea of building an airplane, ship, or even a house in which two-thirds of the volume or up to one-fourth of the floor space was practically not used. In industrial construction given the existing approach to design such a phenomenon has become the norm."[21]

We have revealed the situation with bridge cranes in such detail in order to demonstrate how archaic industrial design in the USSR influences the technology and methods of construction. The technological scheme adopted and the equipment used predetermine the massiveness of production structures, the properties of building components, and, thus, construction materials.

One of the consequences of the demands of technical progress under conditions of competition within and between countries was a striving to synchronize the service lives of buildings and basic technological equipment in industrially developed countries, and this, in turn, gave rise to the idea of the "flexible shop" and the corresponding type of building.

Constructing lighter types of buildings became possible because of the wide use of new construction materials, light and cheap construction and protective building components of prefabricated and collapsible elements. In connection with this there was a sharp increase in the use of light panels of aluminum, asbestos-cement and steel sheets with foam rubber insulation, glass-fiber slabs and other light fillers.

It is difficult to say just what is the first cause: whether routine design in the USSR does not stimulate the development of contemporary construction components and materials or, just the opposite,

---

[21]S. Bulgakov, "Nyzhny novye tipy promyshlennykh zdanii," *EKO*, no. 9, 1980, p. 17.

materials hinders progress in the design of industrial enterprises. These phenomena are interconnected.

But we will try to vindicate the designers and examine just what the possibilities are for using light metal components, polymers, and other modern construction materials in construction.

Soviet specialists recognize the need to change the structure of building materials used in construction, to reject the hypertrophy of prefabricated concrete, and to widely introduce light metal construction components. In characterizing the effectiveness of such a restructuring, Academician Nikolai Mel'nikov presents the following data: light components make it possible to reduce total building mass by 4-5 times in comparison with reinforced concrete, to reduce labor expenditures on outer walls by 10-30 times, and to reduce labor expenditures on support structures and the roof of a building by 1.3-1.5 times.[22] The author devotes special attention to the advantages of aluminum and its alloys as a base material for the production of construction components in comparison with prefabricated concrete.

However, in the sense of steel, aluminum, and chemical products availability, the Soviet construction industry is on starvation rations. According to the estimate of the USSR Minister of Construction, G. Karavaev, construction's requirements for progressive construction components and materials is only 30-40% satisfied.[23] The use of components, parts, and materials from mineral raw materials predominates. In the final analysis, everything boils down to the sharp and growing deficit of high quality steel and aluminum, and this shortage is forecast to continue the 1980s. In Mel'nikov's opinion the production of such steel should be tripled (or more) in comparison with the existing level in order to fully satisfy construction's requirements. With respect to aluminum construction components, they began to be produced only in the first half of the 1970s, and they are much less used in the USSR than in industrially developed coutries. The decline in metal production in the USSR, beginning at the end of the 1970s, does not promise an optmistic future for the construction industry. The only hope is imports.

Such are the deep-seated factors underlying the crisis in construction technology and very substantially affecting the effectiveness of the entire investment sphere of the Soviet economy.

[22]N. Mel'nikov, "Ekonomiia metalla, vyigrysh vo vremeni," *EKO*, no. 9, 1980, p. 5.
[23]*Kommunist*, no. 16, 1980, p. 65.

4. IMPACT OF OBSOLETE CONSTRUCTION TECHNOLOGY ON SIBERIA

The symptoms of Soviet industrial design and construction technology examined above are characteristic of investment activity in Siberia to a still greater extent. Bulky buildings and structures erected on the basis of standard designs of heavy reinforced concrete components and almost without consideration of natural, climatic, and economic particulars have a pernicious effect on the growth rates and effectiveness of Siberian construction and, ultimately, on the realization of plans for the industrialization of Siberia.

In Siberia as in no other region of the country there is a need for designs adapted to specific conditions and for labor-saving, modern construction technology. It would seem that precisely Siberia should serve as the proving ground for experimenting with all sorts of innovations in the construction industry. However, new materials and components are invented, developed, and introduced primarily in the cities of the European part of the country.

In the northern zone of Siberia, the use of heavy reinforced concrete components is stipulated for carcasses, roofs, and other building elements in the majority (80-90%) of designs.[24] Outer walls of brick or cement block are used in about half of all designs. In spite of the wealth of timber in many of these regions, the use of wood components is stipulated very rarely.

The use of steel and aluminum components and wall materials in the northern regions of Siberia provides a much greater effect than in other regions of the USSR. There, one-story buildings comprise about 80% of all floor space of industrial buildings.[25] And it is precisely in this type of building that the use of all-steel carcasses and light outer-wall components, galvanized steel roofs insulated with foam rubber, and aluminum panels in place of reinforced concrete make it possible to greatly reduce the cost and shorten construction time. The use of wood in place of reinforced concrete in these regions is much more economical. The high effectiveness of such construction technology is proved by construction experience in northern regions of Canada and the United States where reinforced concrete has been almost entirely supplanted by light materials and components shipped in and by wood. The use of such materials and components with a high degree of factory preparation justifies the use of air transport to deliver them to the construction site. Assembling them does not require a complicated

---

[24]V. Sarychev and V. Gladkova, "Sovershenstvovanie proektnykh reshenii v promyshlennom i transportnom stroitel'stve," *Problemy Severa*, p. 43.
[25]Ibid., p. 44.

crane system, a large stock of vehicles, or a large number of construction workers. But in northeast regions of the USSR, in spite of the special natural, climatic, and transport conditions, almost the same types of construction components and materials are used as in central regions, and above all reinforced concrete.

According to Academician Mel'nikov's data, experience with the use of aluminum components under northern conditions in Siberia (Dikson, Mirnyi, Chukotka, and Magadansk oblast) showed that in comparison with traditional construction components, the mass buildings was reduced by a factor of 20, the volume of shipments by 10-15 times, construction time was reduced by a factor of four and labor expenditures by a factor of five; the cost of construction of one square meter of production floor space was reduced by 50%.[26]

However, aluminum and steel components are used to a very insignificant extent in construction in the northeastern regions. Reinforced concrete components play the leading role, and the share of metal components in the total volume of construction materials used in the northern part of West Siberia at the end of the 1970's was only 0.3%.[27] Even in the main point of the country's current investment activity—the construction of the oil-gas complex in the north of Tiumen oblast—reinforced concrete dominates. Here is what a well-known Soviet specialist in the area of the economics of construction writes about this:

> That reinforced concrete has been adopted as the leading material also in the construction of the Tiumen oblast oil-gas complex, where the lack of roads, swampy land, and weak ground foundations create great difficulties in the use and shipment of sites of heavy reinforced concrete components, is a matter of concern. Wood materials that are traditional for Siberia are almost not used. For example, in Tobol'sk residential buildings are constructed from panels shipped thousands of kilometers from Omsk; at the same time the wood from the area cleared for the construction site is not used.[28]

At the same time as the volume of construction in Siberia grows and the region's share in construction output of the USSR significantly increase, as does its share of reinforced concrete consumption, production of the latter is concentrated in the European part of the country

---

[26] *EKO*, no. 9, 1980, p. 11.
[27] I. Kariagin, V. Bulatov ad V. Tandalov, *Razvitie gazovoi promyshlennosti severa Tiumenskoi oblast*, p. 43.
[28] *Planovoe khoziaistvo*, no. 3, 1980, pp. 46-47.

(72.6% in 1977). At the end of the 1970s Siberia's share of investment in the national economy was 20%, while its share of production of reinforced concrete was 10%. Production of reinforced concrete per ruble of construction work in Siberia is half that in European regions of the country.[29] It is natural, therefore, that in 1975 80% of the reinforced concrete used in Tiumen oblast was shipped in to supply the colossal scale of construction and, accordingly, consumption of reinforced concrete that is characteristic of that region.[30]

Given such a shortage of reinforced concrete and such a spatial polarization in its production and consumption, a huge quantity of this heavy, difficult to transport material is shipped for distances measured in several thousands of kilometers in spite of the near absence of normal roads and means of transportation suitable to the task. The shipping of reinforced concrete components in these regions diverts 3-9 times more workers for transportation than for carrying out the construction work itself.[31] Transportation expenditures greatly exceed the cost of production. Thus, the production of construction materials and components for the industrial development of the Medvezh'e (Tiumen oblast) gas deposits cost an average of 52 rubles per ton and shipments to the site almost 93 rubles.[32]

Thus, the mass use of prefabricated concrete and the absolutely inadequate production and use of light metal and aluminum components and modern construction materials is one of the basic obstacles to realizing Siberia's investment programs. How much are they aware of this situation in the USSR? Can we expect that substantial changes for the better will be implemented in the foreseeable future and that construction in Siberia will get a new intensifying impulse?

The problems examined above are well known to the leaders of the Soviet construction industry. Already in the early 1970s the author of this work repeatedly participated in sessions at Gosplan, Gosstroi, and the Ministry of the Construction Materials Industry where decisions were made about changing the structure of construction components in favor of metal, about rejecting the universal use of prefabricated concrete, etc. The economic expediency of using steel components in place of reinforced concrete in northern and hard to reach regions had already been proved, and "Technical Rules" had already been elaborated and published, which stated that design and construction

---

[29]G. Tersh, *Material'naia baza stroitel'stva*, Moscow, Ekonomika, 1979, pp. 109-111.
[30]R. Samuseva, *Perspektivnoe planirovanie razvitiia regional'nogo stroitel'nogo kompleksa (na primere Tiumenskoi oblasti)*, Moscow, Stroiizdat, 1979, p. 122.
[31]*Problemy Severa*, p. 56
[32]I. Kariagin, V. Bulatov and V. Tandalov, *Razvitie gazovoi promyshlennosti severa Tiumenskoi oblasti*, p. 39.

organizations, in erecting industrial buildings and structures on permafrost ground and in hard to reach areas, should use steel components, light roofs and walls from galvanized steel, aluminum sheets, and asbestos-cement slabs.[33]

However, to this day little has changed and, judging from numerous sources, the intensive use of reinforced concrete in these regions continues. What are the reasons for such a situation?

The first and main reason was already mentioned: the growing shortage of quality steel and rolled metals, production of which is declining. Increases in the production of chemical products and raw materials for the production of polymer construction materials are also falling. The increase in the production of synthetic resins and plastics in the second half of the 1970s fell in comparison with the first half of the decade by 32%.[34]

Another reason is mentioned by the author cited above, Victor Krasovskii:

> The preferential use of heavy components in construction, and above all heavy reinforced concrete which accounts for 35-40% of the value of all materials consumed, is explained not so much by economical or technical necessity as by narrow branch interests. As we know the overwhelming part of prefabricated concrete is produced at enterprises of contract construction ministries. The price of prefabricated concrete has provided for a comparatively high enterprise profitability—about 20-25% and higher. Until recently the cost of reinforced concrete was included in the fulfillment of plans for construction-assembly work which, in turn, stimulated the preferential use of specifically this heavy and expensive material.[35]

Krasovskii also informs us that more than 2,000 prefabricated concrete plants are in operation in regions of concentrated construction and that the volume of production of reinforced concrete in the USSR is much higher than in the U.S. or in all European countries combined. However, construction ministries plan a still greater increase in the construction of such plants, i.e., a still greater increase in the production of reinforced concrete in the future.

---

[33] *Tekhnicheskie pravila po ekonomnomu raskhodovaniiu osnovnykh stroitel'nykh materialov*, Moscow, Stroiizdat, 1973.
[34] *Narakhoz SSR v 1980*, p. 163.
[35] *Planovoe khoziaistvo*, no. 3, 1980, p. 46.

5. OBSOLETE FORMS OF ORGANIZATION OF CONSTRUCTION

It is not only the fact that designs and construction technology employed in Siberia are unsuited that slows the execution of investment programs there. A no smaller share of the shortcomings is due to transferring to newly developing Siberian regions the methods of organization of constructing that are in effect in the old economically developed regions of the European zone of the country.

As a result of the extending of organizational cliches to the developing regions of Siberia, the basic organizational unit of construction work is the "general construction" trust—a general contractor that as a rule includes dozens of varied projects in its work program. Such a trust is not so much an organizer of the construction of all these projects with the aid of specialized subcontracting organizations as it is a universal performer of almost all types of work. It is a stationary combine of production and transportation enterprises located in a particular place.

As a rule, such trusts functioning in major industrial regions always find work for themselves. The need for their services in such regions is always great—demand exceeds the possibility of satisfying it with contracts. After being created initially to carry out some sort of major project, they shift after it is over to other, usually no less large-scale, tasks. For example, the giant *Kuibyshevgidrostroi* construction trust, after carrying out the basic part of the work on the construction of the Kuybyshev hydroelectric station, was shifted to the construction of the Volga Automobile Plant located in the same region. Incidentally, the decision to locate the plant in this place (Tol'yatty) was determined to a significant extent by the existence there of a ready-made, large-scale construction organization that was capable of constructing an automobile giant.

Transferring the form of organization of construction that had proven itself under conditions existing in urban industrial agglomerations to the developing regions of Siberia has a number of serious consequences for many spheres of the economies of these developing regions.

In the initial period of creation of an industrial center, a stationary construction trust is not only the leading but the only economic organization that devotes any interest to the development of an infrastructure, to its scale and nature. Since construction workers comprise the permanent population, nodal industrial developments are from the very beginning subject to the danger of despecialization and spontaneous growth that far exceeds the limits of the initial design. The projected structure of production, both basic and auxiliary, the optimal number of populated sites and the population distribution plan, the scale and development of the social infrastructure, and, above all, housing construction are all deformed under the influence of the self-generating, expanding construction complex. The real needs of the construction trust, which are auxiliary to its functional role of organization, often displace some of the requirements of basic producers. The development of cities contrary to initial plans is determined in such cases not by the functioning of future enterprises but by the level of construction activity at the time of the maximum scale of its work. In order to support this level, more and more new construction projects with no direct relation to its primary specialization are included in the scheme of the industrial center.

Thus, a tendency develops for Siberian cities to grow out of proportion to the future requirements of normal exploitation of the developing region's resources. Bratsk is an example of this sort of spontaneous development. The same thing is happening now in Nizhnevartovsk and in other cities of developing regions.[36]

Another factor of an organizational nature that has a significant impact on the progress of construction in Siberia is the scattering of construction work among many specialized construction ministries and the absence of a single regional organ that can direct or correct the execution of construction work regulate relations between contractors and sub-contractors, and possess real power in the distribution of resources.

The essence of the branch system of administration of the economy of the USSR is that the decisions made by branch ministries are egotistically oriented only toward the effect within the framework of the branch. No large-scale decision can be implemented other than through the system of branch ministries. Therefore, projects that fall outside the circle of interests of branch ministries lose priority. It is much more difficult to implement them in spite of energetic intervention by central government or party organizations. At the same time, experience with the *sovnarkhozy* showed that shifting the accent from the branch principle to the regional does not solve the problem but modifies it. To date no way has been found to break this vicious circle.

Arguments about the need to develop a fundamentally new system of administration for long-term investment programs of the type involved in developing the West Siberian oil and gas deposits have appeared in the works of Soviet economists.[37] Here it is emphasized that this should not be a branch administration, since enterprises and organizations of many industrial and construction ministries participate in such a program, but it should also not be a regional administration,

---

[36] V. Pushkarev, "Nekotorye problemy formirovaniia Nizhnevartovskogo prmyshlennogo uzla," *Izvestiia Sibirskogo otdeleniia AN SSSR, seriia obshchestvennykh nauk*, no. 1, vypusk 1, 1976.

[37] *Ekonomicheskie problemy razvitiia Sibiri*, p. 219.

since as a rule such a program spreads over the territory of several regions, and its design and implementation involves enterprises and organizations located in various places. Most often this new principle of administration is called "program." However, all these theoretical arguments are of a very general nature, are far from practice, and have not found and, indeed, cannot find any real application.

Thus, no clear impression of some sort of proportional distribution of administrative functions between branch ministries and regional organs exists at present. The primacy of branch administration remains the main principle of economic administration. And while the theoreticians of Soviet science of administration struggle over a solution to this unsolvable problem, numerous ministries, each in its own manner, create numerous construction trusts on Siberian territory, none in any way connected wth the other, and each with its own construction base, transportation and repair enterprises, housing, hospitals, stores, and cafeterias, in other words, as disintegrated as possible both in the production sphere and in the sphere of infrastructure.

Here, for example, is how the Tobol'sk petrochemical combine— one of the most important projects in Siberia—was constructed. The combine was designed as a "model project" that used the latest achievements of both Soviet and foreign (imported) chemical technology and machine-building. Upon the completion of construction this combine will be the largest petrochemical association in the USSR. But at the end of construction is still a long way off: construction work is extremely dispersed. Sixteen ministries are involved in building the combine, while construction is directly carried out by four general contractors (Ministry of the Construction Industry, Ministry of Transport Construction, Ministry of Power and Electrification, and Ministry of Construction-Assembly Work), each of which has its own large construction organization. Labor and material-technical resources are scattered among many construction organizations. It is impossible to concentrate them under one head on some most important top priority projects. They are dispersed absolutely irrationally from the standpoint of the normal schedule and order of work envisioned in the design of the construction process. Investments that have been put into operation starting in 1974 through 1980 are only 70% of the planned level.[38] And this is an example typical of Siberian construction.

It is important to note that this sort of construction organization accumulates its own autonomous infrastructure and strives to expand and increase its share in the distribution of labor material resources. This practice aggravates the already severe shortage of labor and makes

---

[38] *Sibir' v edinom narodnokhoziaistvennom komplekse*, p. 206.

construction in Siberia take longer and cost more.

Organizational forms of construction in Siberia do not correspond to the specifics of construction production in the region. Large construction organizations are justified in constructing enterprises on the scale of the Tobol'sk combine cited above. But departmental dispersion and the absence of a single head dictates their low effectiveness.

The creation of long-term stationary construction bases in areas of new natural resource development, where mobile forms of construction organization oriented toward relatively small volumes of work are needed, is absolutely not justified by any sort of economic experience.

GENERAL OBSERVATIONS

Basic trends in the economic development of the Soviet east and the growing dependence of Siberia on the western regions of the country given the current transportation situation.

A dilemma arises in the practice of Soviet planning in determining the strategy of development for new regions: to form the new element only as a narrowly oriented part of the entire economic system of the country, completely dependent on it, or to give this new formation a definite functional completeness and a sufficient degree of internal stability while preserving specialization in a few products.

To date the first alternative has always been victorious. It is possible to see in this a manifestation of a definite policy which has at its basis a striving to integrate the various regions of the empire. This is undoubtedly correct when the regions at issue are national republics (Uzbek, Lithuanian, etc.) where aspiration to economic autarchy is decisively suppressed. But, in our opinion, this feature of Soviet policy in the area of regional economics should not be used to explain the practice of economic development of the eastern outskirts of Russia, populated primarily by Russians with insignificant disseminations of national minorities. In these regions there are no political or nationality grounds for centripetal forces to arise. At the same time, arguments of a military-strategic nature should induce Soviet strategists to create autonomous economic regions—an idea that to some extent found expression in so-called "territorial production complexes."

Every argument about high expedience always fell into the background when faced with the immediate need for the rapid satisfaction of acute requirements for some sort of raw material, a metal, or fuel, whether it was Kolyma gold during the war years or Tiumen oil and gas in our day. Such a narrowly directed tactic, which in essence boils down to pumping out unique resources with a barbarian attitude toward the ecological problems of the region determines the "point" character of the development of the unsettled territories of Siberia.

In generalized form, the basic features of this type of development of new regions are the following:

1. A single-product, or nearly so, orientation to production in each region.

2. Forced development and exploitation of specialized production and the subordination of all material and labor resources to this. This involves a sharp lag in the infrastructure.

3. A striving for the fastest and cheapest development of the social infrastructure without regard to the future.

4. Even temporary expansion of the output of products of specialization receives priority in comparison with measures and investments of a long-range nature. In other words, the primacy of production over reproduction is clearly manifested.

5. A new region requires ever growing investments, and the effectiveness of additional investments begins to decline quickly due to the need that develops to move on to the exploitation of more difficult to reach or less rich deposits. These difficulties are aggravated by the lags in the infrastructure.

As a result of this sort of development, the living requirements of the new region are supplied by shipments from other regions of the country. As the new region develops and its population grows, its infrastructure lags still further behind needs, and the demand for imported goods from other regions becomes more extensive and diverse. The extent to which the region supplies its own needs grows little. The dependence on other regions increases at the same time that transportation, especially main lines (east-west) become a bottleneck in the country's economy.

According to data for 1975 for Siberia as a whole, consumption exceeded production for gross product, for total industrial output and for ferrous metallurgy, machine-building, construction materials, light, and food industries.

In 1970 for East Siberia, imports of various types of freight from the European part of the USSR amounted to 50 percent of the total weight of freight received.[39] Here it is worth noting that the average price of imported freight was two and a half times higher than the average price of exported freight, and the most expensive goods are shipped into East Siberia from the farthest European regions: Central, Baltic, and Transcaucasus. The largest part of imports (about 80 percent) are

---

[39]L. Legkostup and O. Suslova, "Ispol'zovanie mezhotraslevykh balansov v anlize vosproizvodstvennykh proportsii ekonomiki Sibiri," *Izvestiia Sibirskogo otdeleniia AN SSSR, seriia obshchestvennykh nauk*, no. 11, vypusk 3, 1979.

products of machine-building, light, and food industries.

But it should be kept in mind that the rapid increase in freight shipments and the volumes shipped do not correspond to the developments of the transportation network. Moreover, a growing lag is observed between the development of transportation arteries and the economy's requirements: during the 1960s for each 1 percent increase in gross social product there was a 0.81 percent increase in all dry-land transportation arteries in the USSR; for 1971-75, this figure was 0.78 percent. For each 1 percent increase in freight shipped by railroad, truck, and pipeline, the length of arteries increased by 0.85 percent in 1961-70 and by 0.66 percent in 1971-75.[40]

In this connection it seems appropriate to characterize briefly the specifics of the transportation situation in the USSR.

The principal difference in the transportation situation in the USSR is that, unlike the leading Western countries, it cannot make large-scale use of ocean shipping for raw materials and fuel. As is well known, the intensive use of the raw material and fuel resources of a significant part of the world to a substantial degree became possible and economically justified for the industrially developed countries of the West thanks to the widespread use of ocean shipping by specialized fleets. At present, the local shipment of ores by rail even for a short distance is significantly more expensive than shipping them a long distance by sea.

A particular feature of the USSR is the unavoidability of long distance dry-land shipments. The USSR cannot replace overland shipments by ocean shipping to the extent that Western countries can since it must be oriented primarily toward drawing into use its own resources located deep within the continent. Also to be considered is the fact that the basic ocean coastline of the USSR that provides an exist from the newly developing regions supplying the increase in production of oil and many raw materials is free of ice for only a short time during the year.

In spite of the progress attained in the development of pipeline transport, the main role in the transportation system of the USSR in the foreseeable future will be retained by railroads. Railroads lay the main role in transcontinental freight shipments between Siberia and the western regions of the USSR. It is well known that railroad transportation in the USSR is in a very difficult situation. And this relates first of all to Siberia, where the length of the rail network amounts to 10 percent of the total for the USSR as a whole, while Siberia is involved in

---

[40]S. Kheinman, "Razdelenie truda i razvitie infrastruktury," *Kommunist*, no. 17, 1979, p. 53.

17 percent of all freight shipments in the country.[41]

Here it is appropriate to emphasize that the transport system in the USSR differs sharply from that in the U.S. both in structure and in rate of development. During the quarter century after 1950, the length of dry-land arteries of all types increased by almost three times in the USSR and by only 50 percent in the U.S. But already in 1950 the U.S. had transport arteries with a length 4.3 times greater than in the USSR in 1975. During 1950-75 the increment in the length the over-land transportation network of the U.S. was more than three times greater than in the USSR.[42]

The throughput capacity of rail and truck transportation in the USSR lags further and further behind the growing transcontinental freight flow (in 1971-75 alone shipments of fuel freight from east to west doubled), and the transportation difficulties in the country are growing. The difficult situation with rail transport, its inability to cope with freight volumes that are growing in a geometric progression, is in many cases a reason for the increasingly frequent idleness of plants in the western regions of the country due to shortages of raw materials and fuel from the east and for the halting of construction of enterprises in the east due to failures to receive machinery and equipment from the west. The circulatory system of a giant organism skips a beat ever more frequently; the load on it is too great.

---

[41] *Sibir' v edinom narodnokhoziaistvennom komplekse*, p. 213.
[42] *EKO*, no. 1, 1981, p. 77.

CONCLUSION

As these essays have argued, the current investment policy contributes to the deteriorating conditions of the Soviet economy.

The decline in increments to gross social product and national income, the impossibility of increasing the share of capital accumulation in national income at the expense of consumption due to the danger of internal political complications (the spectre of events in Poland must certainly make the Soviet rulers uneasy), and the need to increase investment in agriculture and transportation—these are the main factors that govern investment policy in Soviet industry at present and, apparently, will continue to shape it in the near future.

An important feature of the investment process in industry is the significant and accelerating decline in the share of capital investment for expansion and, correspondingly, the growth of the share for replacement in gross capital investment. The exacerbation of these factors in the second half of the 1970s is the result of above-optimal rates of growth of fixed capital over a long period of time and a system of depreciation rates that encourage ignoring the objective need for a modern renewal of fixed capital.

Under the existing conditions the main direction of industrial investment policy has been a strict limitation on investment in new construction and a shifting of investment resources primarily to renovation and the development of existing enterprises. Implementing these ideas is seen as a panacea for all ailments of the investment sphere and, above all, as a decisive condition for reducing capital expenditures per unit increase in output. An increasing number of enterprises without the appropriate technological or economic prerequisites is being drawn into the sphere of renovation and expansion.

The idea is to minimize expenditures on updating the so-called "passive" part of fixed capital (industrial buildings and structures), and the major effort is toward updating production equipment. This situation is explained by the following circumstances.

As a rule, the extent to which fixed assets are retired and replaced during the renovation of enterprises exceeds all plan projections and makes the calculations of efficiency, which underly the decision to allocate capital investment for reconstruction, unrealistic. The increase in the amount of assets written off is due to the introduction of new, higher depreciation rates in 1975 and to the reduction of the share of capital repair in these rates and a proportional increase in the share of renovation. The accumulation for several decades of old, overamortized assets due to insufficient retirements, failure to observe depreciation rates, and the economically unjustified hypertrophy of repair to keep assets in working conditions, i.e., the continuing violation of the laws of developing and maintaining fixed capital in pursuit of high rates of growth—all this is manifested in the 70s with the emphasis on reconstruction of enterprises. It is impossible to implement in most cases without fundamentally updating industrial structures as well as productive equipment. The inevitability of the massive replacement of assets, especially the passive component, is the rock that is holding industry down in its efforts to achieve capital-saving increments to production at existing enterprises.

The key point of renovating existing enterprises is to update equipment to a new, substantially more progressive technical level. But this is also not sufficiently realized. Machine-building industry does not have the scientific and production potential to quantitatively and qualitatively satisfy the growing requirements of enterprises undergoing renovation. Improvements in the technical level of newly installed equipment are lagging further and further behind the growth of fixed capital (in constant prices). The number of new models of equipment developed is declining. A quite significant trend is emerging: the cost of new equipment is growing faster than its productivity.

Soviet industry has achieved more in the way of quantitative results through renovation than qualitative results. The output of renovated enterprises is more likely to be improved than qualitatively new. New enterprises are better suited for creating fundamentally new equipment. Therefore, a reduction in investment in new construction, all other things being equal, narrows the possibilities for creating new technology that uses new energy and raw materials resources (not only the most abundant) but has different qualitative features. This has the effect of reducing technological progress. Thus, a vicious circle is created: the greater the share of industrial investments are put into existing enterprises, the less are the possibilities for carrying it out effectively on a fundamentally new technological basis that ensures savings of capital and labor resources while increasing the volume of output.

In light of these facts there is reason to conclude that the growing trend toward priority investment in existing facilities will not lead to a quicker return on investment and will not create the prerequisites for raising production growth rates, but will slow down technological progress in the Soviet economy. The phenomena that have been noted will become more widespread in the foreseeable future since long-term investment policy in the Soviet Union is based on increasing the share of investment in existing production.

As we examine the Soviet investment program for the 1980s—at least for the first half of the decade—we can see that it is riddled with confusion and contradictions. For every one of its theses, there is an

antithesis:
- On the one hand, the leadership plans to increase the share of consumption in total national income and proclaims the primacy of social programs; on the other, they plan to reduce further the share of investment in housing and services, which had already reached a record low in the late 1970s.
- On the one hand, the plan calls for maximizing the percentage of investment in existing industry, most of which is situated in the European part of the country; on the other, it calls for the transfer of funds to the northeast in connection with the new investment impulse aimed at increasing the production, transport, and processing of oil and gas, and at development of the associated infrastructure. Shifts in the regional structure of capital investment which occurred in the second half of the 1970s testify to the fact that this second alternative has already started to be realized.
- On the one hand, investment in the so-called fuel and energy complex has sharply increased; on the other, investment in the industries which create the foundation for the development of this complex has slowed.
- On the one hand, investment resources are to be concentrated on almost-completed construction projects, which will provoke a sharp increase in the demand for equipment; on the other, there is no commensurate increase in the share of investment going to the machine-building industry, even though in recent years there has been a fall in output and in the number of new productive capacities put into operation for many kinds of equipment.

In a word, one cannot really speak of an "investment strategy" in the foreseeable future. The investment activity reflects the rate of emergency existing in the Soviet economy, and is subordinated to the pressing need to leave untrammeled those branches of the economy generating foreign exchange and those producing arms.

* * * * *

The decline in the investment resources of the economy as a whole and the reorientation toward replacement and the development of existing facilities significantly limits the regional maneuverability of investment policy in the USSR. While the overwhelming majority of raw material and energy resources are concentrated in the Asiatic part of the country and especially in the northeast, the spatial distribution of capital investment continues its primary orientation toward European regions where 80 percent of industrial production and the largest part of the manufacturing industry is concentrated. Renovation of industry in the European regions absorbs a growing part of capital investment and been necessary to divert ever greater proportions of capital resources to the extractive sector of the economy. Crucial here is the fact that the extraction of raw materials and fuel places a far higher demand on capital and labor than does manufacturing.

The predominance of extractive industry and primary-stage industry for processing raw materials is steadily increasing, and this has given a primitive cast to Sovieet industrial production. The result, indeed, has been a vicious circle: the more that resources are diverted to maintaining and accelerating the production of raw materials and fuels, the less that can be allocated for the development and production of new producer goods and technology. And the more that the producer goods and technology fall behind modern standards, the more the raw materials and fuels that are required for per unit production, and hence the still greater demand for more fuels and raw materials.

* * * * * *

Under all these conditions, the need to force investments onto Siberia presents the Soviet ruler with a fatal challenge.

At present there are two tasks on the agenda stimulating the Soviet leadership to expand investment in Siberia. The first is to increase the production for internal consumption and export of Siberian raw materials, primarily fuels, in order to import vitally necessary goods. Second is to strengthen the military-industry potential of Siberia in case of a world war or a military conflict with China.

The economic situation in the USSR and the external political situation are pushing the Soviet leadership to solve these two supertasks at any price and in the shortest time possible. The development of Siberia is being carried out not on a broad front, not on a planned basis, and not in accordance with any long-range strategy, but on an emergency basis, spasmodically, ignoring the region's interests as an independent economic system, and with a predatory attitude its natural resources and maintaining an ecological balance.

As a result, growth rates of production are slowing and the disproportions in Siberia's industry are deepening. Extractive industry is becoming more cut off from manufacturing, and the economic dependence of Siberia on western regions is growing.

Under the existing conditions the Soviet leadership objectively cannot shift still greater investment resources to the industrial development of Siberia since the industrial base in the western part of the country is in such a difficult state and requires ever increasing resources in order to maintain the existing level of production.

But even these additional resources would be useless at present; the resources that are being allocated are not being used efficiently because the industrial structure of Siberia (like, incidentally, that of the entire country) is not prepared in either an organizational or scientific-technical sense to implement such a large-scale investment program. There is not sufficient labor. The capacity of the construction industry and the condition of the construction base in no way measure up to the tasks with which they are faced.

Economic development of Siberia at accelerated rates is not a local task but a decisive condition for supporting the economy of the entire country. It is appropriate to recall Lomonosov's prophecy: "The might of Russia will be increased by Siberia and the Northern Ocean."

* * * * * *

We can now say that the reality of Soviet investment goes against the structural changes in the industry which are necessary for rejuvenation of the economy. Of course, a forecast for development of trends described in this book is feasible only in the context of a general politico-economic forecast for the whole Soviet system. This writer never set such ambitious goals. It can only be said here that in realizing the need for major long-term investment programs with different leading branches, the Soviet rulers cannot look beyond the framework of their short-term impulsive decisions in making their investment policy. All this requires radical, resourceful steps. But so far the current leadership has done nothing more than to run in place.

CODA

The essays have pointed to some basic structural problems in the Soviet economy. It should be clear that these are *structural* problems and that, consequently, only changes in the basic economic structure can lead to a resolution of the country's economic difficulties. One can hardly overestimate the enormous efforts, the scope of internal and foreign policy compromises, that are required if Soviet leadership is to overcome the inertia directing Soviet economic development for more than half a century. Time is not on the side of procrastination; the longer decisions are deferred, the more difficult and painful they become to solve.

Hopes for the sufficient impulse for an upsurge in investment for the accelerated development of the industrial potential, for the smoothing out of disproportions in the economy, can arise only if the Soviet leadership, under the threat of ruin and economic collapse, accepts compromises both in internal and external policy, reduces military expenditures, and receives Western credits.

A political metamorphosis of this magnitude, however, would require a kind of decisiveness and courage which can scarcely be expected from the current leadership. If, however, the current (or more likely, the next) generation of Soviet leaders concludes that genuine reform is inevitable in order to reinvigorate the economy, they will have no choice but to adopt far-reaching structural changes, especially in the area of investment policy.

hinders its redistribution in favor of eastern regions.

This trend in the regional distribution of investment contributes to the growing spatial gap between the concentrations of raw material and energy resources and their users and processors. The growing polarization of the location of the extractive and manufacturing branches of industry on the vast territory of the USSR creates an excessive burden on the entire transportation system and especially on the main railroad arteries, whose condition is deteriorating sharply and whose development is lagging behind the requirements of the economy.

Investment in the industrial development of eastern regions is more and more concentrated on the primary goal—accelerating the production of raw material and energy resources. This orientation of investment flows results in a worsening of the disproportions in the economies of eastern regions between the development of the basic industries of national specialization and the auxiliary service links of the economy (construction, transportation, etc.). The social infrastructure and, above all, housing construction lags further and further behind the growth of the productive sphere of the economy. This distortion in investment in the economic development of eastern regions creates a growing difficulty for carrying out construction and production programs in their basic sectors.

These difficulties are due to the insufficient potential of the construction sector, the poor condition of the transportation network, and the lag in the construction of housing and other components of the social infrastructure behind the population's needs. The latter circumstance is a decisive factor in the growing labor deficit in the most important regions of industrial development in Siberia and the Far East. The existing order of priority in Soviet investment practice when developing new regions—the primary orientation toward creating basic production facilities to the detriment of the development of infrastructure—is clearly manifested currently in the development of the oil and gas deposits of West Siberia. The violation of normal proportions for the harmonious development of territorial-production complexes in less developed regions in pursuit of the quickest possible expansion of capacity in a region's specialized production strikes the main goal like a boomerang—it constrains the growth of output causing underfulfillment of plans. But the point is not only that the rate of growth of manufacturing branches and the productive and nonproductive infrastructure is lagging behind the growth of extractive branches. This phenomenon is not specific to the development of pioneering regions only in the USSR. The more important point is that the narrowing of the spectrum of investment activity in the eastern regions because of the investment stress in the nation's economy and the continuing priority given to western regions in the regional distribution of capital investment contributes to a slowing of the shift in the regional structure of manufacturing industry and electric power to the east.

The greatest task, whose fulfillment hinders the spatial orientation of capital investment outlined above, is the regional deconcentration of industrial production as a military strategic factor. During the entire history of the development of the USSR, in the event of war the Soviet rulers have painfully felt the vulnerability of the economy of a huge country to a high degree of spatial concentration of industry. Precisely for this reason an attempt was made to improve the distribution of the military-industrial potential. In particular, this goal was the basis for making the decision about investing in the construction of the Ural-Kuznets combine or the creation of an aviation and shipbuilding industry in the Far East at the end of the 1920s and the beginning of the 1930s. The extensive investment program in the 1950s and 1960s to create the Angara-Yenisei complex, a new energy base for the eastern part of the country, was essentially determined by this factor. The need for comprehensive development and settlement of the eastern border regions is dictated by the strategic military interests of the USSR. However, investment efforts were never significant enough to overcome the age-old trend in the geography of Russian industry.

The collision between the realization of the need to implement a long-term investment program of regional deconcentration of manufacturing industry and comprehensive development of eastern regions on the one hand, and investment to achieve the short-term goal of a maximum increase in the volume of production in existing industry of western regions on the other, was always the main contradiction of the regional aspect of investment policy in Soviet industry. This contradiction has become especially acute now as a result of the investment slump and the increasing spatial polarization of the extraction and manufacturing branches of industry.

* * * *

The fundamental fact in Soviet economic development has been the hypertrophied development of extractive and raw materials production, which is caused by almost exclusive orientation its own natural resources.

In addition to the orientation on domestic resources alone, another cause of structural imbalance in the economy is the low technological level for the utilization and processing of raw materials and fuels—an inefficiency, in other words, that leads to increased demand.

But to sustain and accelerate this growth rate in the extractive sector (which not only satisfies the increasing demand of the Soviet economy, but its increasing volume of export trade in raw materials), it has